Niel Pendleton has been involved in fund raising for 35 years from coast to coast and overseas. He has lectured on fund raising at Harvard University's Center for Lifelong Learning and has contributed his efforts to churches, independent schools, hospitals, and a college seeking to raise funds.

To
Jim
my son
1939~1979

Fund Raising

A Guide for Non-Profit Organizations

NIEL PENDLETON

A SPECTRUM BOOK

PRENTICE-HALL, INC., Englewood Cliffs, New Jersey 07632

Library of Congress Cataloging in Publication Data

Pendleton, Othniel Alsop (date)
   Fund raising, a guide for non-profit organizations.

   (A Spectrum Book)
   Bibliography: p.
   Includes index.
   1. Fund raising—United States.   I. Title.
HV41.P39   658.1'5224'0973   80–26950
ISBN 0–13–332163–0
ISBN 0–13–332155-X (pbk.)

A SPECTRUM BOOK

10 9 8 7 6 5 4 3 2 1

Printed in the United States of America

PRENTICE-HALL INTERNATIONAL, INC., *London*
PRENTICE-HALL OF AUSTRALIA PTY. LIMITED, *Sydney*
PRENTICE-HALL OF CANADA, LTD., *Toronto*
PRENTICE-HALL OF INDIA PRIVATE LIMITED, *New Delhi*
PRENTICE-HALL OF JAPAN, INC., *Tokyo*
PRENTICE-HALL OF SOUTHEAST ASIA PTE. LTD., *Singapore*
WHITEHALL BOOKS LIMITED, *Wellington, New Zealand*

Contents

Foreword

If fund raising has not yet become a science, it is surely an art in the hands of the more gifted professionals. Readers of this book are placing themselves under the tutelage of a mature and talented practitioner of the art.

The special virtue of this book is that it is written from a perspective that is at one and the same time humanistic and practical. I have come to know Niel Pendleton as a man who cares deeply about institutions and the people who are served by them. Fund raising is for him an act of thoughtful service which helps sustain socially valuable institutions and programs and at the same time enriches the giver by drawing him into a process that transcends himself.

This small guidebook reflects a thoughtful set of values and encapsulates a lifetime of hard-won experience and carefully refined insight into the behavior of organizations and individuals. For several years Niel has offered intensive fund raising workshops at Harvard University's Center for Lifelong Learning and his efforts have always been very well received both in terms of the formal evaluations of his courses and in the subsequent testimony of those who have applied what they learned from him. It is pleasing to see that what we have offered at the Center is now available to a wider audience.

Jeremy W. Rusk, Director
Center for Lifelong Learning
Harvard University

Preface

Many excellent ideas in the realm of education or social welfare die before fruition because of lack of financial resources. Many small organizations, dedicated to the improvement of some segment of society, struggle with inadequate program and staff because they do not know how to raise larger funds. Hundreds of groups which were once adequately financed, often by endowments, now are being forced to search for newer sources of support.

This book is designed to assist these nonprofit organizations in uncovering funds to strengthen both new and established enterprises for the good of society.

My four years teaching at Harvard University's Center for Lifelong Learning introduced me to scores of persons engaged in independent education, in ecology, in museums and the arts, in work with ex-convicts, in providing housing and more adequate dieting for handicapped children. All have high dreams. All are busy at tasks that will benefit other people. All are seeking assistance.

I am grateful for the many who have helped me over the past four decades in the art of fund raising, especially to leaders in the American Baptist Churches, the United Church of Christ, the United Presbyterian Church in the U.S.A., and the Episcopal Diocese of Western Massachusetts. The fund-raising firm of Marts and Lundy gave me basic training and impressed me with their sense of service. Jeremy Rusk provided the teacher's dais at Harvard. In these classes I have had the valuable help of Alfred Gibbens, William Boardman, Michael Boland, Susan Hendrix, Richard Flood,

Loomis Patrick, John King, John Kerr, Jeanne Brodeur, Julia Sinclair, Edward Metcalf, Richard Boardman, and Michael Hurley. Readers of the manuscript for this book have been Julia Sinclair, Michael Boland, and William Haney.

For quotations or source material I am indebted to John Kerr, Austin McClain, Burr Gibson, Robert Lazear, Mariam Noland, Haney Associates, Covenant Presbyterian Church (Fort Myers, Florida), many other churches, the Harvard Business Review, *Fortune Magazine*, and the Kresge Foundation. Also to the Kingswood School of West Hartford and the YWCA of Hartford, Connecticut.

Jeanne Brodeur was kind enough to write most of the material dealing with direct mail.

It has been a pleasure working with Mary Kennan, Alberta Boddy, and Pat Lewis of Prentice-Hall, Inc. and Wilma Kilgore of Kingsport Press.

Niel Pendleton
Westwood, Mass.

Introduction
So you want to raise funds!

The genesis of modern fund raising came from two men working separately several hundred miles apart as YMCA secretaries in the 1890s, Lyman L. Pierce and Charles S. Ward. By 1905 the two pioneers had joined forces to launch a million dollar campaign for a new YMCA building in the nation's capital. It was purposely designed to demonstrate to the country what could be done. The public period of the campaign was squeezed to one week to enhance the drama. As a result, when World War I struck, the talents of the professional fund-raising counsel were at hand to direct the huge war bond drives.

Over two generations of experience have resulted in a body of knowledge that has been proved in the crucible, and now been adopted by thousands of institutions and causes in America, and elsewhere.

Although the steps and techniques of these sixty years of experience are seen in finest flower in the intensive capital fund campaign, they have been adapted by annual and occasional drives, much to their strengthening.

This book will serve the purpose of the cause seeking either capital or annual funds. It is intended to assist both the novice and the seasoned professional. The beginner in fund raising will have here a guide, whether he or she be associated with an established institution or setting up a promotional plan for some new cause. The experienced development officer will find here an overview of campaigning, drawing together principles and methods that will provide both a refresher and a reminder. This book should be especially helpful to all whose institution chooses to campaign without benefit of a professional fund-raising firm. Trustees, administration, and volunteers will discover the various steps required for an effective drive, and how these steps are coordinated. Here are tested methods, which, if given into the hands of persons willing to devote long and devoted hours, will lead to exciting results.

The more experienced, more competent, practitioners in this field believe this work to be a profession. Though it has not been widely accepted as such in all circles, we believe it is well on its way to such acceptance.

To those who are new to this work, whether you are engaged by the most prestigious hospital in the state or to some small group of neighbors resolved to improve some condition in life, I say: Congratulations!

You are in for an exhilarating experience if you know what you are doing, and can obtain competent volunteer help. On the other hand, you will encounter frustration if everything you attempt is on a trial-and-error method. Such procedure will set you on the road to failure, or at least to only moderate success.

The purpose of this book is to set forth time-tested concepts and methods so that every worthy, nonprofit organization may achieve in quick order a strengthening of its financial undergirding.

No other country in the world has so developed the concept of voluntary organizations to improve society as has the United States. And, it follows, no other nation is so advanced in the field of voluntary fund raising. American citizens are proud of their nongovernmental institutions to ameliorate conditions of distress, to improve health and culture, and to educate the ignorant. And we are proud of the vital role we play when asked to assist in raising money to support these enterprises.

Congratulations to us all!

It was a fund-raising assignment that began the twenty-year climb of James H. Evans to chairmanship of the board of Union Pacific. As vice-president of Dun and Bradstreet, Evans was given the task of soliciting corporate gifts for the American Red Cross in New York City. He raised $3.6 million, impressing E. Roland Harriman, then national chairman of the Red Cross. Thus did the son of a poor Kentucky Baptist preacher become the protégé of the son of one of the railroad magnates of the nineteenth century. Harriman, in time, recommended Evans for the presidency of the Seaman's Bank for Savings. Shortly thereafter Harriman again recommended Evans, this time as a director of the Union Pacific board, since he "has done such a swell job for us at Red Cross and could do the same for the railroad." From there Evans became number two man for the transportation company and in 1977 the chairman.*

There are many ways to raise money for a good cause—bingo, charity events, ticket-selling, inducements to giving (prizes, etc.) or outright giving without any benefits to the donor except a sense of partnership in a worthy enterprise. This book will deal only with the latter. Everything we have to say will be based upon the premise that America (above all other nations) is filled with citizens who believe in giving a helping hand, and who want to be co-workers in an enterprise that promises to bring about social improvement. Alexis de Tocqueville, in *Democracy in America,* wrote of this American trait a century and a half ago. It is still true today.

Our task is to organize this good will.

* From FORTUNE magazine, August 1977, p. 17. © 1977 Time, Inc. All rights reserved. (Reprinted by permission).

CHAPTER 1

Where is your organization in fund raising?

Regardless of whether your organization was established only last month or has been raising funds for over a century, you can be helped:

– by reviewing what other groups have been doing
– by surveying the broad field of fund-raising techniques
– and by looking at fund raising in its entirety as a basic tool in the ongoing battle against ignorance and man's inhumanity to man.

IS YOUR ORGANIZATION BRAND NEW?

Many societies—or often only one person or a married couple—become possessed with an idea. How best can we aid in helping disadvantaged children, elderly people, eradicating a disease, rehabilitating newly released prisoners, rebuilding lives crippled by drugs, saving a redwood forest or an endangered seashore? The list is endless.

Thom Hartmann's organization stood at almost ground zero. But he had a driving passion. He knew he had to do something about helping troubled children. For one thing, a friend had pestered him into taking a quick, sudden trip to Germany to see what Gottfried Muller was doing in his three Salem Children's Villages.

1

For another thing, Thom had spent time as a fifteen-year-old locked up in a children's institution as a runaway.

So he sold his three businesses, which employed seventeen workers, and headed with his wife, Louise, and two children to New Hampshire to see what he might do. The only backing, besides his personal slim resources, was a $5,000 start-up loan from the West German organization and some expense money.

Thom's basic idea was that children need love, the love that shines most brightly in homes or homelike settings. Out of this can grow a child's sense of self-worth. His second idea was that poor nutrition is often an important factor in children's behavior problems, an idea inherited from Muller and endorsed by Dr. Ben Feingold. Thom and Louise bought a house and within two weeks there was a phone call. A state social worker was calling: "I hear," she said, "that you are beginning a home for children. I need help. I have with me three children I must place tonight. I do not know where to go. Will you take them in?" The Hartmanns did, and that was the beginning. Today there are thirteen children in the home, located on a lake-front farm in Rumney, together with seven houseparents, two cooks, and a volunteer construction crew of six.

Thom came to my class in fund raising at Harvard, eager for help in solving some of his problems, primarily financial. They seemed well nigh insurmountable at the time. But Thom and Louise are making progress. The Governor of New Hampshire has commended their work. Their expenditures have exceeded $100,000 annually. But income seems to hover around the $90,000 figure. "Consequently," says Thom, "I spend a lot of time knocking on doors."

There are hundreds of similarly motivated people in America. And thousands of social welfare and educational institutions struggling with vision, but lacking expertise in financing their ideals.

IS YOUR ORGANIZATION WELL ESTABLISHED—BUT WITHOUT AN ADEQUATE FINANCIAL PROGRAM?

The changing economic and sociological patterns in America—soaring inflation, fear of "boom or bust," decreasing family size—have forced institutions hitherto secure in their financial undergirding to reassess their structure and to look for new sources of support. This time of soul-searching can result in much advance. For as these troubled institutions look about, they discover not only that their own objectives call for reappraisal, but that other groups—other causes—have led the way through the labyrinth of finding new friends and larger dollars. Experience of others has much to teach us.

DOES YOUR ORGANIZATION WITH A WELL-CONCEIVED AND EXECUTED FUNDING PROGRAM FEEL THE NEED FOR REVIEW— FOR DEEPER SELF-ANALYSIS?

Most of your program may be proceeding quite satisfactorily in the eyes of some. Yet you wonder whether too close attention to daily chores may lead to astigmatism. Or perhaps you have forgotten something that you once did and now need to reinstate. Or you need to keep abreast of what others are doing in the field of fund raising.

This guidebook is designed with each of these three types of institutions in mind.

BASIC QUESTIONS

Once you have decided on action, there are certain basic questions you must keep asking if you seek the help of other people.

1. Do you have a board of trustees or directors who help you determine policy and objectives? See Chapter Four.
2. Have you looked into receiving a state nonprofit corporation charter? Have you applied for IRS tax exemption? To receive this you must prove that you are a publicly-supported institution (that more than one-third of your income comes from the public). Then you fill out IRS Form 1023, followed perhaps by Form 990. Finally, your organization will be listed in the U.S. Treasury's *Cumulative List of Organizations.* Guidelines are in the IRS publication 557 and Package 1023. Without these steps, your donors may not be able to declare their gifts as deductibles from their taxes.
3. Have your objectives been clearly spelled out? Can you reduce your purpose to one paragraph—not more than one-half sheet of paper? See Chapter Eleven.

4. Are you willing to seek the help of other people in refining this statement of purpose? And later seeking their advice as you move ahead? See Chapters Four and Seventeen.

5. What is your timetable in reaching your goal? Few organizations are able to finish their fund raising job in the time originally set. So be prepared to extend your deadlines. And after you are sure that you are ready, can you be sure that your constituency is ready? See Chapters Eight and Ten.

6. What are the items you must spend most of your fund raising budget on? Which items the least? See Chapter Nine.

7. How large—and how rich in potential—is your list of would-be donors? See Chapter Fifteen.

8. Have you determined to have an annual appeal or a drive to raise one large block of funds? See Chapter Two.

CHAPTER 2

Capital campaign, annual appeal, or both?

Are you going to set up a capital campaign, an annual appeal, or a combination of the two, conducted at the same time? Do not confuse the two.

The capital campaign seeks to raise money for new or remodeled buildings, or for land, or for endowment. It usually seeks pledges payable over a period of three years, and occurs only once or twice in a decade. It solicits larger individual gifts than does the annual drive and has a greater dollar goal. It seldom, or never, includes items for maintenance, salaries, or programs, and if it does, it is only for a limited start-up period.

The annual appeal raises funds for current operations for one year and is repeated every twelve months. It does not attempt to underwrite major building programs or build up endowments.

The newly established group or society must not think of either a capital or annual appeal, but of an ongoing solicitation until such time as an adequate list of supporters is built up. Only then does it begin to make its appeal annual. Once a society has established a base, it should not ask for funds in every mailing. To do so means that after a while its constituency will cease to read its mailings. Get your appeals onto an annual basis—except for the occasional large gift—as quickly as possible. Then your mailings can emphasize accomplishments and news with the appeal being indirect and subtle.

Each of these two types of campaign has its advantages, and

each aids the other. The capital campaign requires longer-range planning, greater detail work, and often, the use of volunteer solicitors. General principles are the same for each type of campaign, but some of the steps of the capital can be eliminated from the annual.

This book will set forth the principles and techniques derived from the capital campaign. It will then indicate where adaptations can, or should, be made for the annual appeal. Bear in mind, however, that the closer the annual fund sticks to the sixteen steps, the greater the results. Time, manpower, or budget will prevent your following each step every year. But you would be well advised to vary your technique somewhat from year to year, letting the sixteen steps guide you in choosing not only which steps or techniques to omit but also which to put into your program this year, to be deleted or modified two or three years from now.

The annual appeal forces you to go out every year to build up your prospect list. It gives you a listing of dependable donors— those you can count upon to give from year to year. Your roster of supporters should be thought of as in three categories:

– those giving virtually every year
– those giving sporatically
– those who have not yet given but are capable of larger gifts if and when interested.

This third grouping you must continually build up and cultivate as to what your cause is. If you do not enlist them for annual gifts, you may be able to obtain gifts for a capital thrust at some future date. There are some development officers who state that the ultimate purpose of a capital campaign is to increase greatly the number of annual contributors.

The annual appeal prepares the way for the capital drive. The capital campaign strengthens the annual drive.

The two methods of fund raising by capital drives and annual appeals are not the only sources of donations, particularly for educational institutions and museums. There is the bequest, which can be handsome indeed, and is generally thought of as the way to build up endowment. Then there is the occasional large gift, outside of either type of campaign, which may come from individual, corporation, or foundation.

It has been stated that, over a broad spectrum of educational institutions and a wide span of years, donations will fall into these categories:

How received:	% of total amount of giving:
annual fund	10%
individual large gifts	20%
bequests	20%
capital funds campaign	50%

The size of the donation to the capital effort cannot be judged solely by the size of the annual gift. Keep in mind that there is always the possibility of a "once-in-a-lifetime" gift or a "twice- or thrice-in-a-lifetime" gift. Thus, someone who gives you $25 or $100 a year may be motivated to make a major capital gift of $10,000 or $100,000, depending on many variable factors. The good fund raiser is ever alert to this possibility.

The capital campaign, dealing with such high goals and requiring unusual amounts of volunteer service, is best when directed by an outside fund raising firm. The concentration of effort, the time-bind which forbids most trial and error (and, indeed, most hesitation), and the need to enlist and train the huge number of volunteer callers required, would advise against the capital campaign being run by the usual staff. Professional fund raisers are not cheap. Neither are lawyers and doctors. But each group is experienced, and it is in the intensive drive for maximum dollars that experience pays off.

If you decide on professional help, keep in mind a maxim of fund raisers: "A campaign is as good as the person assigned to it."

CHAPTER 3

Role of the development director as counselor

The role of the development director tends to be that of a background person. The director must shun the spotlight, avoid getting his or her name and picture into print. Let credit be given to the chief executive and, most important, to the volunteers. The director is an enabler—one who, realizing the paramount importance of the volunteers, enables them to perform their fund raising assignments with ease and dispatch. The director does not solicit, but prepares the way for the solicitor, who may be the head of your organization or a volunteer. The director follows up, seeing that the call is completed and the donor thanked. The director conserves the time of the president, freeing him or her from piddling details and protecting the president from undue demands.

ATTRIBUTES OF THE FUND RAISER

The effective fund raiser is one who likes people and enjoys working with them. A good fund raiser has a basic understanding of human nature, and, without getting bogged down in the latest popular psychology trend, knows something of the art of giving and asking. The fund raiser needs to be deeply interested in the cause for which he or she works, for only belief in the validity of this cause will lead to that degree of sincerity which others will recognize. Integrity, then, is a sine qua non of fund raising for educational and philanthropic work.

An organizer, adept at handling innumerable details, the good fund raiser knows how to delegate, and to supervise. This is a person who can plan ahead and will not be sidetracked by incidental events.

This person has a love of language and some facility in expression. His or her memos and instructions will be clearly stated.

Delighting in solving problems, the effective fund raiser does not hesitate to seek counsel from cohorts, but also knows when to cut off discussion and get into action.

A healthy respect for research is invaluable. This work the director oftens assigns to staff, but one must know what to look for, and how to express the findings in a layperson's language.

It is expected that one will quickly become knowledgeable about the cause or institution represented. The fund raiser needs to be acquainted with some historical background, with current problems, and with financial details. This person must quickly gain a picture of the mission of the entire institution.

The fund raiser is to be facile in presenting knowledge of the appeal he or she is engaged in. One need not be a polished speaker (though it helps), but must be expert in knowing how to present knowledge in visual or aural form.

One must take pride in this type of work and be willing to spend many midnight hours upon it.

Gently aggressive the director must be in prodding others to perform the task assigned, in promoting the cause, and in seeking gifts. Abrasive one cannot be, but forthright and persistent and courageous (at least a modicum). This person must put aside fears of offending, convinced that the value of the cause is self-evident and will carry the day against timidity and delay.

Does the fund raiser know how to listen? If not, he or she had better learn. I once called, with a young associate, upon a clergyman to seek his advice on securing a large gift for a mission enterprise from a wealthy member of his congregation. The proposed donor was reputed to be the wealthiest woman in the state, and we knew the minister's cooperation was essential. He received us graciously, and seated before a wood burning fire in his Elizabethan study he began telling us a story about the donor. In the midst of the story my associate interrupted: "Doctor, can you help us get a gift?" It was evident he had not been listening. The clergyman's mouth dropped, his eyes showed injury. He was crestfallen. "Joe," I scolded, "the doctor has not finished his story. I want to hear the rest of it." The clergyman recovered, finished the story, and in due course, the denomination received a sizable gift, a gift almost lost by inattention.

It is a primary rule that in fund raising one's attitude must always be positive. One must never apologize in asking support for a worthy, well-administered cause. The development director takes the lead in expressing a positive attitude and then seeing that his or her campaign leaders do likewise.

In a church campaign in Fort Myers, Florida, to pay off a mortage—a drive that would save the church at least $130,000 in interest charges—the chairman, Bob Rockwell, was a highly successful developer of land and condominiums. Bob was a born leader, an aggressive salesperson, and a committed church member. At our very first meeting, less than twenty hours after my arrival, with twenty-five church leaders in the room, Bob made a statement about it being too bad that we had to ask for money. Now this was a crucial moment. How positive—or negative—would these leaders be at the very beginning of our drive? I found it necessary to interrupt. With a big grin, and a friendly touch on his shoulder, I said: "No, Bob, we are not sorry to have to ask for money. We are proud to give, and to ask others to give, for in our giving we are building the Kingdom of God." Bob has since become one of my good friends.

People want to be associated with a successful project. They want to feel that they are co-workers in an enterprise that betters the lot of humanity. Such co-work requires time and money. Leaders must not have a negative attitude. Do not apologize in asking for time or money.

FINDING A FUND RAISER TO EMPLOY

I once asked a young man engaged by a college to raise funds: "How did the college find you?" "An ad in a Sunday newspaper. 'Wanted, Development Director,' it read. So I turned to my roommate: 'What is a development director?' He explained. I answered the ad and was invited for an interview. In the conversation the president and I talked about Emily Dickinson, Henry Thoreau, and Herman Melville. After an hour of this, to my astonishment, the president said: 'You are hired.'" The young man lasted less than a year.

The headmaster of an independent school had a better idea. At a conference on fund raising he said: "If I had in my budget a certain figure for salary of a development person, I would not put it all into the salary of one person. I would instead choose a recent bright college graduate at a modest salary and spend the remainder on counseling by a fund-raising firm."

Finding a competent fund raiser is not an easy task, primarily because there is no readily available source of supply. There is nothing similar to an engineering or law school to satisfy the needs of those professions. There are a few, very few, universities or schools which give degrees, or college credit, for courses in fund raising. This is helpful, yet it is generally felt that the art of fund raising cannot be so much taught as learned by experience. This means that organizations are often reduced to raiding staffs of competitors.

Institutions can train their own personnel, though the difficulty is that too often neither the president nor anyone else associated with the institution has either the time or the know-how to devote to such training. Too much is expected and too little guidance is given. That is why so many new fund raisers last two years or less in their jobs. It is a procedure that is expensive to the institution and unfair to the young person.

Perhaps the most effective way to train neophytes has been to employ them as assistants in a capital drive directed by a professional firm. In this way the young person receives an intensive course in the complexities of fund raising from an experienced professional who soon will be leaving.

FINDING A PROFESSIONAL FIRM OR PERSON

Most capital campaigns get direction from a professional—either a firm or an entrepreneur. The stakes are too high for the institution or agency to do otherwise. When one is engaged in an effort calling for time of a year or more, along with its demands upon staff and budget, and the price of failure or semisuccess in the eyes of the constituency, it is rash not to consider "outside help." Put very simply, there is not enough time to experiment to find out what works. The organization must know where it is going and how to get there. Often the outside professional is the only one possessing sufficient know-how. But there is another consideration: sometimes there are persons within the organization who have the knowledge but who, in an intensive campaign, do not possess enough clout to implement their knowledge.

The question then becomes: Where does one find such direction?

The oldest and largest organization of fund raising firms is the American Association of Fund Raising Counsel, 500 Fifth Avenue, New York, N.Y., 10036. Besides being a clearing house for some of the largest firms in the country, this association has also testified before government bodies concerning legislation to improve and regulate this fast-growing field. The association will send a listing of member firms. They publish, among other pieces, the much quoted annual, *Giving USA,* a storehouse of facts and figures on educational and philanthropic giving each year in America. Not all fund raising firms belong. There are firms which once belonged and no longer do, and there are others which have never joined. Some of these may serve your purpose. In every case obtain a list of recent clients and inquire by telephone as to their satisfaction.

The National Society of Fund Raisers is a much less formal grouping of individuals who join either as staff members of a grant-seeking organization or as independent fund raisers. They have societies in a number of states and several major cities, meeting every one or two months. If you can find them, they may be able to provide some professional suggestions for you. There are some experienced individuals or very small organizations who can be very helpful. Here again, ask some former client by telephone about performance.

How does a professional firm or individual work? They do not solicit for you. They do not work on commission. They will agree with your organization ahead of time as to how much time they will supply, how much workforce, some idea of your goal, and what the costs will be. They then conduct some type of feasibility study, define campaign objectives, prepare schedules and guidelines, write publicity, recruit and train the volunteers who do the actual soliciting, and attend to records and reporting. No ethical fund raiser will "guarantee" any goal. This person can only offer you experience, judgment, and the ability to work hard. Though a professional may appear to be expensive, he or she is usually one of the best investments the institution can make.

DUTIES OF THE FUND RAISER

One of the early duties of the fund raiser is to clarify roles—to assure that all understand the role of the professional and this person's relationship both to staff and volunteers. The fact that the director does not actually solicit individual gifts may need to be stated again to all involved. The director is a counselor, a preparer, a coordinator with these primary tasks:

- Directs the fund raising staff, assigning responsibilities, checking quality, correcting defects and omissions.
- Devises a master plan and draws up all calendars and schedules.

- Guards the budget and confers, ahead of spending, with trustees or administration over major adjustments necessary in the budget.
- Presents the strongest, most appealing statement of your case.
- Will help find prospects, and then supervises the rating and assigning of them.
- Writes whatever materials your staff cannot handle; prepares study books, manuals, information sheets, newsletters.
- Prepares instructions on how to make a solicitation.
- Selects foundations and corporations as potentials, researching them, and preparing proposals.
- Advises on adjustments to the goal and how to report amounts received.
- Supervises the enlistment and training of callers.
- Keeps abreast of happenings in business, government, legislation, and rival institutions.
- Are special events to be part of your drive? The development director will plan and execute them.
- Analyzes the campaign step by step and submits written reports. (This person will be a master of detail).
- Sets up proper records and arranges a collection system for payment of pledges.
- Provides forthright constructive criticism of others and, in turn, will be grateful for constructive criticism.

HELPS FOR THE DEVELOPMENT DIRECTOR

There are available for today's fund raiser a plethora of written material. These range from autobiographies of philanthropists to recollections of outstanding fund raisers, from studies on modern-day philanthropy to the psychology of giving, from periodical publications on techniques to advertisements on available materials.

The merest sampling of books include: Allan Nevins: *Study in Power—John D. Rockefeller;* Edgar J. Goodspeed: *As I Remember;* William Lawrence: *Memoirs of a Happy Life;* Cleveland Amory: *The Proper Bostonians;* E. Digby Baltzell: *Puritan Boston and Quaker Philadelphia.* Then there are various accounts of university fund raising efforts, particularly of Yale, Princeton, and Stanford, often found in alumni magazines.

There are magazines on fund raising. Two of them are: *Philanthropy Monthly,* published at New Milford, Connecticut, 06776 (Box 989) at $36 per year, and *Fund Raising Management,* a bimonthly costing $12 per year, published by Hoke Communications, 224 Seventh Street, Garden City, N.Y. 11530. An excellent new periodical is the monthly newsletter produced by the Lutheran Resources Commission, Suite 823, 1346 Connecticut Avenue, Washington, D.C. 20036. It runs about thirty pages, typed, and costs $50 per year. *The Grants Magazine* is a quarterly addressed both to the grant seeker and the grant maker. It is published by Plenum Publishing Corporation, 227 W. 17 Street, New York, N.Y. 10011, and costs $45 per year for institutions and $22.50 for individuals.

Keeping up to date with foundation trends can be obtained by reading annual reports of the larger foundations (free for the asking) and the various publications of the Foundation Center in New York City.

Trends in federal government grants can be gleaned from various official publications. Of especial interest may be the productions of HEW, of the National Endowment for the Arts, and the National Endowment for the Humanities.

Among the private organizations interested in grants is the Council for Financial Aid to Education 680 Fifth Avenue, New York, N.Y., 10019. They have many studies dealing with giving of corporations to education.

In the 1950s the United Presbyterian Church in the U.S.A. was engaged in a drive called the Fifty Million Fund. Two problems were outstanding: inducing the ministers of local churches to lead their churches in taking part, and influencing the members to make their own gifts. Austin McClain, chief counselor for the national drive, summed up the task of the area fund raisers in a statement that is true for all types of fund raising:

> Our job is to solve problems. We do far more than raise money. People do not like to give. Neither do they like to solicit. People give to people. They want to help solve a problem. They do not give to a Fifty Million Fund.
>
> The question we need to ask potential givers is: "Are you in favor of helping build a hospital in Africa?"
>
> We can help ministers by urging them to take leadership. The minister should say to his church: "Let's go."
>
> The pastor's position in his church is strengthened if he takes a strong position of leadership. This is especially true in giving leadership to the Fifty Million Fund.
>
> AUSTIN MCCLAIN, former chairman of the board of Marts and Lundy, Inc., and consultant to Lehigh University

CHAPTER 4

Role of the trustee

A board of trustees, sometimes called board of managers, board of directors, or board of overseers, is essential for any body which seeks funds from the public.

Trustees are the permanent guardians of an institution. It is they, rather than the administrator, who determine policy and thus set the general course that the institution follows. They write, and amend, the constitution and bylaws. They compose the statement of purpose. They appoint—and dismiss—the administrator. They determine, or at least approve, the budget. The trustees decide whether property is to be bought or sold, and whether to enter into capital campaigns.

The Pacific School of Religion was without a president in the autumn of 1977, when I was invited to assist in a campaign to raise funds to supplement a foundation grant for erecting a new building. It quickly became apparent that the constituency (including some of the trustees) were not willing to give in large amounts until the future direction of the graduate school was clearly determined. This would best be accomplished by a rewriting of the seminary's statement of purpose, plus the choice of a new president.

As I prodded the administrators and nearby board members to redraft the statement of purpose, a debate arose. "We should wait," said several trustees, "until the president is selected and ask him or her to do so." But, meanwhile, the pressure was on the building committee, on the finance committee, and on me to quickly raise the additional funds, since groundbreaking was soon to occur.

For over two months the debate continued until it was finally resolved by Daniel Aldrich, Chancellor of the University of California at Irvine, a seminary trustee, who declared:

> "We the trustees are the permanent guardians of the institution. It is up to us to determine the course of the school, and then to see that the president and staff and faculty conform to this statement of purpose."

Trustees are essential to protect staff from lawsuits.

Trustees give a seal of approval to an organization. They reveal to the public who is behind the institution, who is the guiding hand. A board of recognized, eminent trustees gives validity to the institution and to the work it is doing.

Trustees assist and guide the administrator in making the tough decisions. They stand between the staff and their critics when decisions are made that may not be popular. They are a support to the chief fund raisers of the institution. This begins with the trustee, the giving of his or her own time and money. It extends to the trustee's circle of acquaintances, influencing them to make donations from time to time. The conscientious trustee is willing to approach corporations, foundations, or government agencies for grants. The trustee is capable of—and willing to—lead in fund raising endeavors. Should there be no trustee capable of heading a financial drive, he or she will be able to recruit some prominent person not on the board to give voluntary direction.

The smaller, or newer, organization often does not have the leadership on the board of directors or sufficient strength, or experience, to lead a drive for community support. In this case, a committee of the board must seek outside help. If they do not know whom to ask, they consult with bankers, lawyers, and leading business persons as to whom they recommend.

From 1973 to 1977 the budget of the Alvin Ailey American Dance Theatre catapulted from $700,000 to almost $2,700,000. But such growth made heavy demands upon the time of Alvin Ailey, time which he would rather have spent in creating a new dance. Ailey's problem arose in part from his selection of a board—the highest talent from the black community, but persons without wealth. Survival came only when the board members pledged personal guaranties to the banks of amounts from $750 to $5,000. Then came a reorganization of the board to include persons of wealth.

Newer, smaller organizations usually find it difficult, if not impossible, to enlist persons of wealth to serve on boards. Yet the attempt should be made, for wealth attracts money. If you are unable to persuade affluent persons to serve on your board, then strive to enlist leaders of the community—persons who will have access to persons of means.

Does your board need strengthening? How do you go about it? You must begin with the head of your institution and the present chairperson of the board. Let them seek the advice of four or five present trustees at a luncheon meeting. Do *not* discuss this matter before the entire board. In most cases the administrator or chairperson must personally invite the prospective trustee to serve. This invitation must never be done by letter or telephone. Only a personal call suffices for this crucial assignment.

You never "fire" a trusteee. Most organizations have limited terms for board members, at the expiration of which (often three years) the unproductive trustee is replaced. Perhaps you should enlarge your present membership. Or create a new, supplemental group, such as "Friends of Your Group." Such an auxiliary could consist of past trustees, potential trustees, and others who may never become trustees but are strong backers of your work.

When Stanford University in 1959 planned to raise $100 million for capital needs, at that time the largest goal ever sought by an educational institution, the trustees agreed not to launch the campaign until they first secured a campaign chairperson who might be able to direct the campaign successfully. It was two years before they found the man they desired, not an alumnus of the university. Their promise to him was that, upon completion of the campaign, they would elect him to their board. This campaign went over the top by $14 million and paved the way for their next campaign which, in 1977, reached $304 million.

A college, or any institution seeking large gifts, must be aware that gifts of magnitude do not come without cultivation of the would-be donor, and often the size of the gift is in proportion to the time and the care exercised in cultivating the prospective benefactor. Oftentimes this cultivation occurs after the person is elected to the board.

The administrator who attempts to make all decisions, without reference to the board, not only is burdening and depriving himself or herself of the wisdom of a group of responsible citizens, but is also guilty of not cultivating the board so that they know they are part of the team, and not mere rubber stamps. Involving directors in decision-making is one of the surest ways to lead to eventual financial participation.

A few years ago I was engaged in running a feasibility study for a proposed capital campaign. After I had interviewed a few lukewarm friends of the institution, one leader bluntly revealed the true situation to me: "That executive," he complained, "wants

to make all the decisions. O.K., then, let him raise his own money."
That campaign was never launched. The cause was worthy. The
friends were financially able. But the administrator had alienated
his own board by not seeking their advice.

Even the oldest of colleges and schools sometimes neglect their
trustees. One of the well known colleges in America embarked on
a capital campaign for $9 million. The first part of the drive was
the identification of all alumni on a regional basis. Annual giving
dominated this first year. The campaign for capital gifts, more low-
key, went on simultaneously. As a result there were double, and
with deferred giving, even triple askings, plus reunion askings. Many
alumni became confused and alienated by the several directions
the college was taking during that inauspicious year.

One of the trustees, a brilliant woman, came into the college
office with questions. Why was the college requesting her to seek
major gifts from people in her area who had made a gift to the
college's annual fund in the range of $5 to $25? A good question.

The problem was that the institution had concentrated on training solicitors in key areas but had neglected to train, advise, or
educate its own trustees. Many who were willing to ask for a substan-
tial gift from alumni who may have, for the most part, been pleased
to contribute, were left on their own, confused and ignored, until
almost too late. Having raised a little over a million dollars the first
year, the college was forced to reconsider its fund raising priorities,
putting a new emphasis upon capital giving.

There was a second problem. Many committees were formed
for the campaign: committees and advisory committees to committees, but few were acutally given anything to do. For the most part
they were not asked for an opinion, and when asked, felt they were
not being heard. Alienated by this approach, many gave less than
they might otherwise have given. It is dangerous to enlist the aid
of volunteers, especially trustees, and then give them nothing to
do, and no guidance.

Ignore your board at your peril.

CHAPTER 5

Role of the volunteer

The use of volunteers in a fund raising operation can greatly facilitate the successful movement of a campaign if properly organized and directed.

Any campaign can become more successful as more details are handled—details such as sufficient mailings to prospects, accurate updating of office records, prompt acknowledgment of donations, and, if gifts are sought by personal approach, reminders and aids to the volunteer workers. Many years of experience, in several different types of drives, emphasizes the observation that extra hours spent in such tasks pay off. Many a good idea has been written down at 3:00 A.M. The question then arises: How can the development director attend to all these additional details? How can he or she be assured of a good night's sleep?

The answer lies in the use of volunteers—volunteers for office work and volunteers for solicitation.

The Bureau of the Census tells us, through the Statistical Abstract of the U.S., that in 1974 there were almost thirty-seven million volunteers in America, unpaid workers serving religion, education, hospitals, civic and community groups, and social and welfare organizations. Forty-two percent of these were between the ages of twenty-five and forty-four, while 27 percent were between forty-five and sixty-four. Only 8 percent were retirees. Here is an illustration of the adage: "If you wish a job well done, ask a busy person."

Let's summarize the reasons for using volunteers in fund raising:

1. You need help. Fund raising calls for many details. You do not have sufficient time to handle them all yourself. Therefore, volunteers multiply your effectiveness.

2. Use of volunteers is a splendid way to cultivate prospects. The more the volunteer gets involved, the more he or she understands, the more enthusiastic he or she becomes. This work may be internal—assistance in office work such as addressing envelopes, inserting mail, revising lists—which is usually done by homemakers or retirees. Or, more important, it may be external—solicitation of donations in eye-to-eye appeal. This is a task usually for the businessman or woman, preferably one who uses salesmanship in one's daily business.

3. Volunteers spread the word as to what you are doing for the community. They are interpreters of your program in the most effective method of communication—person to person.

Do not be misled by the person who says: "I am a poor fund raiser." Dr. Edwin Dunphy, a member of Harvard University's Institute for Learning in Retirement, said that to me and then followed with:

"A few years ago at Massachusetts Eye and Ear Infirmary, I was getting ready to operate on the eyes of a retired man from Ohio. Shortly before the operation he said to me: 'Doctor, I am in the habit every evening of taking two martinis before dinner. I know the use of alcohol is forbidden here. But I am fearful, and it would ease my mind a great deal if you could grant this privilege to me.'

"I was able to make this arrangement, and in due course he was operated on, recovered, and sent home. Not long after he sent a letter to the hospital and one to my medical school—Harvard—expressing appreciation for my work and my concern for him. He wanted, he said, to do something for each institution in honor of me. Enclosed in each letter was a gift of $450,000."

Few persons like to ask for money. It is often difficult for them to do so. But it is fallacious for them to assume: "I am a poor fund raiser."

4. Volunteers are imagemakers. They give creditability to your organization. Few of your public will be able to get a detailed picture of your aims and accomplishments, but they do have confidence in people whom they know and trust. Thus, a common response is: "I do not know that organization personally, but I see that so-and-so is assisting them. Since I have confidence in him or her, I will be favorably disposed to their work." This is the reason why

so many organizations publish on their letterheads and in their publications the names of sponsors and other volunteers. It opens many doors.

5. Volunteers will account for a significant percentage of your financial goal. They tend to be better givers. This is because they understand your program and your problems, and thus are more willing to give. It is a mistake to use as solicitors persons who do not give themselves, for their production record will be minimal. In a capital campaign an executive of a large company offered to enroll fifty or so solicitors for my campaign. I was delighted, for volunteers in a citywide drive can be difficult to obtain. When I walked into the training session, I was elated by the appearance of the volunteers, young, bright, well dressed. But when the chairperson, who had secured these volunteers, announced that we did not expect them to give, I knew that we were in trouble. It later became evident what had happened. These volunteers were present, not because of a desire to help, but because they had been drafted by their bosses on a promise that they would not be asked to give themselves. Results? Less than $100 was raised by this group of fifty. Without their personal commitment, few calls were ever made and no effective solicitation was done.

6. Volunteers are usually a source of enthusiasm. As they give you more time, and thus become more acquainted with your ideals, their interest turns to endorsement and then, hopefully, to enthusiasm. Their devotion is not only infectious to outsiders, it spreads among other volunteers, and even serves to lift the morale of the staff. Many a development director has found renewed strength from the enthusiastic volunteers who, having a different perspective on the accomplishments of the group or institution, bring to him or her words of commendation.

The use of volunteers implies a sharing of decision-making. No group of nonpaid workers can long be kept active without their assuming some responsibility, and thus, eventually, some voice in decision-making. It is this reason why some executives shy away from the volunteer. This is particularly true of the long-term volunteer, such as a member of the board of trustees. This person tends eventually to become powerful in terms of determining policy and sometimes this results, especially in newer organizations, in the board displacing the executive who may have had the original idea and nurtured it through many agonizing months (or years), only to see his or her place, or influence abolished.

Yet the originator of the dream, who first dreamed and then implemented, must be willing to put himself or herself in this position if he or she seeks public support. No one person, no one group, can ask for support and then totally ignore the concerns of the public. The privilege of fund raising is balanced by the sharing of responsibility. There is no other recourse in the long run.

Disadvantages in Using Volunteers

There are some disadvantages in using volunteers. The astute director faces this problem ahead of time and builds safeguards into his or her system. The director does not dismiss the thought of using the volunteer because of certain weaknesses.

The volunteer does not wish to take orders. This person does, however, need and appreciate directions. The fund raiser can give these instructions himself (or delegate them to the secretary) if there be only three or four volunteers. A larger group requires more personal attention, since this size group will include persons without office experience, etc. A most effective method is to appoint one volunteer to supervise the others. Do NOT assume that volunteers will do the job properly without some guidance.

Unless the job for the volunteer is very simple, such as preparing a mailing, any work that requires great speed is usually best done by staff. For most assignments staff will be much more efficient. But they will seldom match the production of a group of volunteers under selected supervision.

Be careful of the nonpaid worker if you are not sure of his or her ability. Tasks demanding great accuracy, or some artistic ability, should not be assigned until the director knows the ability of the volunteers. If the work is poorly done, there is always the "public relations" problem—hurt feelings caused by rejection of the work.

Lack of enthusiasm quickly shows itself in any assignment involving time or care. The executive can often care for this problem beforehand by taking a few moments to thank the workers and stress the significance of the immediate task.

There are, of course, many assignments which the volunteer can do more effectively than any of the staff. Merely be alert to the problem of insufficient time or injudicious selection of workers.

Why do businesspersons give volunteer service and what do they discover in so doing? Dan H. Fenn, Jr., gave the conclusions from interviewing over 400 businesspersons, reported in the *Harvard Business Review* (March/April 1971).* Business executives give

---

* Reprinted by permission of the Harvard Business Review. Adapted from "Executives as community volunteers" by Dan H. Fenn, Jr. (March–April 1971). Copyright © 1971 by the President and Fellows of Harvard College; all rights reserved.

time for various reasons, but many of them summarized their willingness as based upon the belief that the concerns of the organization were the same as theirs, that the work of the agency was badly needed. Some stated that they felt the agency could use their skills. One manager summed it up:

> "Sometimes I wake up early in the morning and wonder what I am really here for. If it isn't to make a contribution, I don't know what it is."

Of those interviewed, 85 percent stated that more businesspersons must become involved and help volunteer organizations. Some felt that their professional jobs were not interesting enough. More than one-third said their companies had written policies stating that pay and promotion were dependent in part on community participation.

Eighty percent of those interviewed disliked token participation, and 83 percent were active in two or more organizations.

Of the active volunteers from business, 65 percent were age forty-six or older. Fifty-seven percent came from large companies while only 16 percent from small companies. The very best leadership was given by businesspersons from top management, the poorest from middle management. In types of industry represented, 60 percent of the volunteers came from service industries and only 23 percent from manufacturing industries.

What did these volunteers discover? Nearly half of them said they were underutilized, that staff did not release enough responsibility to them. There was a great lack of communication between staff and volunteer. Only 15 percent of the volunteers said they were adequately briefed on their task.

The conclusion of Fenn was that organizations need to inform their volunteers more adequately, finding ways to bridge the communication gap. The agency should target their recruiting at the large service companies and pick their desired leadership selectively. Few leaders were true volunteers; they had to be recruited.

The selection of proper volunteer leadership is a key ingredient in the success of any fund raising program. Go for the best available in your community. Inform them fully of aims and procedures. And let them exercise initiative once they are selected.

CHAPTER 6

How to organize the campaign

Your organization—your idea—needs financing. It is, you are convinced, worthy of public support. You have decided to seek contributions.

How do you get started?

There are eight broad areas to which you must devote early attention.

One—determining your need.

You, and others, must give careful thought to why you are seeking funds. You must decide whether your needs are:

A. Operating
    —salaries
    —new equipment
    —annual operating items
        new items or increased amounts
B. Capital
    —remodeling of property
    —new building
    —acquiring additional property
    —endowment

Next, you need to obtain an estimated cost for each item.

You then decide whether to seek these new funds year by year (operating) or by pledges for three or so years (capital). Sometimes there is a melding of the two objectives. This occurs when your operating needs are so great that you are forced to finance them over three years, expending them on a decreasing basis from your newly pledged money until the annual income is able to carry them. Thus, you might spend your new funds: 60 percent the first year, 30 percent the second year, and the remainder the third year. This arrangement calls for increasing the regular annual giving so that it carries these special items in future years.

Two—stating your case.

Once you have determined your needs, you must reduce them to writing. This assignment can be very demanding. The writing must be:

- brief
- clear
- devoid of professional jargon

Your statement must demonstrate that your needs are salable—can the public be persuaded to support your ideas?

Three—finding your prospects.

You now decide to whom to direct your appeal. Who are in a financial position to respond? Who can be influenced to participate? Think in terms of:

- areas
- categories of givers
- relationship of givers to your cause

If your constituency is all in one city or county, your campaign is simpler than when you reach out statewide or nationwide. If your area is widely scattered, plan your drive as a series of local drives beginning with your home base. In other words, first run a campaign in your hometown, then repeat this pattern in as many places as you believe you will find results to be worthwhile.

You must decide whether your support will come from:

- individuals
- corporations
- foundations
- societies or clubs

Each category calls for somewhat different organization and approach.

You need to determine the relationship of prospective donors to your cause, since the organization and publicity may have to be modified somewhat for each type. Thus an educational institution will think of alumni, present parents, past parents, friends. A club or society will think of members, past members, friends, local businesses.

Four—rating the prospects.

If your drive will be seeking an equal amount from each prospect, you need not rate. But this system, usually a direct-mail campaign, calls for extensive mailing lists. Any drive that includes personal solicitation should rate the prospects before the call is made.

Think of your prospective donors as of varying ability and varying interest. The simplest division of your list would be the top 10 percent of more able givers, often called advance givers or special givers, and the remainder ninety percent of general givers. More established institutions will have more elaborate divisions of donors. These few top prospects will give far more than 10 percent of your receipts, provided you set up special types of organization and cultivation to reach them.

Five—setting the goal and budget.

It is harmful to set a goal unrealistically high, since it reduces public confidence in your judgment and tends to work against the morale of staff or board. Your goal should be based upon a consideration of four factors:

- your past record of receiving gifts
- your present need
- the attitude of some of your leading friends, found out through personal interviewing
- your willingness to work hard, enlist helpers, and follow a plan

In setting your campaign budget, see what organization and publicity you can have with a budget of 5 percent of expected funds raised. Established organizations with staffs can finance a campaign with 3 percent or less of money pledged. A less experienced group may need to spend 10 percent. This seems to be a good norm. Avoid going over 20 percent. It is around this point that criticism sets in.

Six—setting up committees.

Your board of trustees may already have, or may wish to appoint, their own standing committee to supervise all fund raising. We recommend this as a permanent body. You will also need a special committee for the campaign itself, particularly if it be a capital drive with pledges payable over three or so years.

Begin by naming a general chairperson for the campaign. Be

sure he or she is an accepted leader in your circle and a generous giver. Then, working with this chairperson, the administrator or a small group of trustees help the chairperson fill the rest of the general committee.

Here is what your campaign organization might look like:

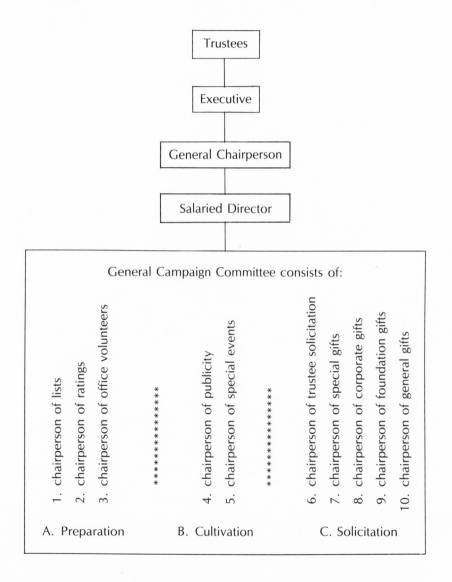

Each chairperson of the ten sections chooses whatever members needed to assist. The largest section, by far, will be section 10—the general gifts workers. See the following chart.

General Gift Chairperson

recruits four:

Division Leader A	Division Leader B	Division Leader C	Division Leader D

Each Division Leader then recruits 4 Key Persons. Total—16 Key Persons. See the following.

Each Division Leader

recruits four:

Key Person A	Key Person B	Key Person C	Key Person D

Each Key Person then recruits 4 Workers. Total—64 workers. See the following.

Each Key Person

recruits four:

Worker A	Worker B	Worker C	Worker D

Since each division leader can cover 100 calls, the preceding chart is sufficient for 400 calls. For each additional 100 calls, add one division. For fewer calls, decrease divisions.

See also Form 18–1.

Seven—drawing up the schedule.

Before embarking on any fund-raising drive, you must make a calendar. Decide on your closing date. Then schedule events backwards to the present. The items which usually take the greatest time are:

– securing the volunteer solicitors
– printing and mailing
– preparing the brochure or mailing piece

It is assumed that the rationale for the campaign—the "why" of the drive, the needs for funds—has been agreed upon before the campaign opens. Otherwise this one item can sometimes consume months of time.

The minimum campaign calendar might well be six weeks. The maximum could be three or four years or more.

Eight—Listing the records and forms needed.

Some records may require a couple of weeks—or much longer—to design and produce. Allow plenty of time by planning ahead and ordering early. The minimum list of forms and records might be the following. Do not hesitate to add others to fill special requirements.

1. Card file of prospects, alphabetical. You may also need a geographical or zip code file.
2. Master list. Your control sheet, which lists names and addresses, the solicitor for each, the amount suggested, the amount pledged. See Form 22–1.
3. Rating lists. Flat lists of prospects, for use when others help you rate giving abilities. See Forms 15–1 and 15–2.
4. Prospective workers lists. To help your leaders secure their workers.
5. Organization chart. See Form 18–1.
6. Pledge cards. In addition to the regular card, you may want a special card for major givers. Forms 19–4, 19–5, and 19–6.
7. A fact sheet for instruction of workers.
8. A question-and-answer sheet, either for workers only, or for broad distribution.
9. Workers' kits. You may need to print a folder which will hold several pieces for use of the worker.
10. Forms on which to record pledges. Forms 22–1 and 22–4.
11. "Thank you" forms. Form 21–1.
12. Forms on which to record payments. Forms 22–2, 22–3, and 22–5.

CHAPTER 7

Sixteen steps: operating procedure

The rest of this book deals with procedures to be followed in raising funds. These procedures have been tested primarily in capital fund raising and are now being adapted to raising annual funds. There are, of course, more times as many annual appeals as there are capital drives. But since the capital campaign is a more thorough drive, requiring in larger drives two or three years or longer, it involves more steps, in far greater detail, than most annual efforts. A study of the procedures of the capital campaign will assist the directors of the annual appeal.

Annual drives do not require all the following steps. But the more of them you use, the stronger your effort will be. Different types of campaigns, together with different personalities of development directors, will lead to great diversity of procedure. In brief, use as many of the following sixteen steps as possible, if not this year, then next year. And vary your drive somewhat from year to year.

One of the purposes in my writing this book is to assist the development director (as well as the administrator and trustees) to see their task in the whole—to fit together all the pieces of their jigsaw puzzle of steps and see what is missing, what is occupying too much time, what calls for more attention.

The work that you and I are doing—improving society through disinterested volunteer service—is too important to be slipshod.

Here are sixteen basic steps of an intensive, time-tested procedure in raising maximum dollars. Think twice before eliminating any one.

Step One—THE FEASIBILITY STUDY. Prepare for your campaign by conducting a preliminary investigation, often called a feasibility study. This survey is an internal review of the fiscal health of your organization, together with a study of past funding operations upon which you may now build. It is also an external inquiry into the feelings of your most influential friends concerning possible goals, timing, and methods. Carefully done, it will save you time, money, and missteps.

Step Two—BUDGETING. Determine ahead of time your budget for the drive. What will you need for salaries, printing, postage, rent, travel, and meals? You must be able to borrow enough to pay costs until fresh funds begin coming in.

Step Three—SCHEDULING. A careful calendar needs to be drawn up. You must determine your closing date and write down each step needed to reach your goal. Be especially alert to allowing sufficient time for writing, printing, assuring proper attendance at key events, and for recruiting the volunteers needed at each level of your campaign organization. It is as important to omit unessential tasks as it is to perform the essential ones.

Step Four—PREPARING THE CASE. You must be able to state the purpose of your drive succinctly and clearly. Attempt to state the "why" of your campaign in two or three paragraphs. This statement requires the approval of your board.

Step Five—SETTING THE GOAL. Beware of setting an unattainable goal. Shun the temptation of going for all you can get. Have a goal that your supporters will be glad to help you reach.

Step Six—COMPILING LISTS. Your prospect list is extremely important. This list must be large enough to allow for many refusals, but even more crucial, it must consist of persons who can become interested in your cause and who are in a financial position to respond.

Step Seven—CORRECTING LISTS. An out-of-date list does you harm, for it is expensive to process, and it can cause resentment, as when one of a married couple has died a while ago. You must devise a process to maintain correct names and addresses.

Step Eight—RATING THE PROSPECTS. Most drives need to distinguish names of more affluent prospects from the less affluent. You will need the help of many persons to rate your lists. You should offer the prospects different dollar levels to which they can respond.

Step Nine—CULTIVATING THE DONOR. Every prospective donor needs information and reminders. It is your duty to tell your story in a fresh, attractive manner.

Step Ten—BUILDING THE ORGANIZATION. After you have determined how to make your appeal (by direct mail, or by radio or television, or especially by eye-to-eye presentation), you then work out the number of volunteers needed. To obtain maximum dollars, you will need many volunteer solicitors.

Step Eleven—RECRUITING WORKERS. The securing of solicitors in a campaign is one of the more difficult jobs. It calls for a pyramiding of workers—one person at the top who enlists a few leaders, who each in turn enlist a few others, who also may have to enlist yet another tier.

Step Twelve—TRAINING WORKERS. It is largely a waste of manpower to send out uninformed volunteers. You must provide not only printed helps, not only oral instructions concerning the aims of your society or work, but also training in the best techniques.

Step Thirteen—SECURING THE GIFT. The call upon the prospect, is of little value if the solicitor does not ask for the gift—gently, courteously, firmly. A few simple techniques have demonstrated their superiority at this crucial point.

Step Fourteen—THANKING THE DONOR. Everyone desires thanks, and the quick acknowledgement is more appreciated than the delayed one. Your system needs to be worked out ahead of time.

Step Fifteen—CLEANING UP AND COLLECTING. Too many drives leave too many incomplete assignments. Those last few calls can often pay the entire cost of the campaign. And inattention to collection of pledges can result in losses of 10 percent or more of your pledges.

Step Sixteen—REPORTING RESULTS. The development officer—or the volunteer directing the campaign—needs to make a final written report to trustees, which can also be a historical record to others. It should include statistics and also comments on the strengths and weaknesses of the drive.

CHAPTER **8**

Step One:

Preparing for the big push: the feasibility study

What are the chances for success of your proposed campaign? Is your contemplated goal too high or too low? Is your timing right? Whom can you count on for top leadership? Answers to these questions are found in the feasibility study. A good study saves time, money, and possible embarrassment if the campaign be ill-considered.

A feasibility study is a survey to determine whether your institution is ready for a major drive for funds, whether your constituency is sympathetic toward your plans and will support you, where your funds are apt to come from, how long a period will be necessary to reach your objective, who might give voluntary leadership, and what size goal you should go for.

All of this takes place BEFORE any announcement of a campaign takes place. In other words, you predetermine your chances of success before you begin action.

Why, you may ask, spend time and money making this survey when the campaign itself will provide the answers?

Because you do not want to have a failure due to your possible constituency knowing too little of your work—or your present plans. Or because your supporters felt that your timing (for many varied reasons) was off.

Or because your organization was not ready, due to inadequate prospect lists, or plans not thoroughly thought out, or lack of proper leadership, or inability to provide proper office space, or lack of funds to launch a drive. Reasons for failure are multitudinous.

Or because you announced a goal so high that your public considered it unattainable and hence refused all but nominal support.

No institution—no society—can afford failure. And no professional fund raiser wishes to be associated with failure.

Suppose your campaign raises 50 or 75 percent of your announced goal. Some insiders may then say: "Well, at least we are that much farther ahead in dollars than we were." But will you be? Who wants to be chairperson of your preordained failure?

But such a campaign is expensive, for a campaign that reaches its goal is no more expensive (indeed, may be less costly) than a drive that falls short.

Furthermore, the effort that reaches its goal builds a sense of achievement, of pride, of confidence in the staff, so that this heightened morale makes the next campaign—whether for annual or capital funds—easier.

And, a successful drive is the best source of good public relations, for it shows the public that you are capable of wise planning and businesslike action. Again, this public approval is the basis for success for your next appeal.

A properly conducted feasibility study will save you time, expenses, and embarrassment. It is preselling of the very best type.

In the two year period 1969–1971, I directed two campaigns, one immediately following the other, in Hartford, Connecticut. Both were successful in their objectives, though each received its funds from different sources. The first one, Kingswood School, obtained virtually all its money from individuals—parents, trustees, friends. The second, YWCA, obtained only 25 percent from individuals, 65 percent from corporations, and 10 percent from foundations. What was it that revealed to us the different procedures that needed to be followed? It was the feasibility study in each case.

HOW IS SUCH A STUDY ACCOMPLISHED?

It is difficult for any group or institution to conduct its own feasibility study. This is because of the lack of objectivity. Since everyone wishes to look good, it is extremely difficult for the administration to reveal conditions in its past record of service that divulge weaknesses. Hence there is an all-too-human tendency to gloss over weaknesses that may, in times of intensive campaigning, seriously hamper the drive.

The staff of the organization finds it difficult to listen—to honestly listen—to any criticism. This may be due in part to the staff's preoccupation with its own aims and deeds. They are so positive of the worthwhileness of their work that they unconsciously reject any criticism. Or perhaps they are fearful of what might be revealed if they probe some sensitive area.

There is a second, perhaps even greater, flaw in a staff-conducted survey. That is the reluctance of most outsiders to find fault—face-to-face—with any staff persons responsible for the workings of the organization.

A feasibility study must be twofold:

– external to determine the attitude of your constituency
– internal to reveal the strengths and weaknesses of the administration as it affects future fund raising.

THE INTERNAL ASPECT OF THE FEASIBILITY STUDY

The internal aspect of the feasibility study will bring out:

– past experiences of fund raising upon which you may now build
– statistics upon which you prognosticate your chances of success
– trends over several years in such areas as:
    balancing of budgets, cash flow, liabilities
    annual fund raising
    capital fund raising
    growth or decline in enrollment of members or students

Statistical tables must be drawn up to reveal trends over the past ten years. Any lesser period is unreliable, since unusual factors in any one or two years may distort the general picture. Compiling ten year tables will show to even the most perceptive administrator where elements of weakness lie. Or, occasionally, it will give heart to leaders who have been so tangled in day-to-day problems that they may have become pessimistic over their true progress.

The forms needed for an internal study will differ with the type of institution or organization. A general guide can be found, however, through studying the forms used in a college or independent school feasibility study.

AREAS OF STUDY FOR
A COLLEGE FEASIBILITY STUDY

1. Distribution of alumni or supporters. This study will show in how many localities the institution should set up area campaigns.
2. Alumni classifications. How many alumni are there? How many are graduates? Concerning other prospects, how many present parents are there? Past parents? Nearby prospects or businesses? Number of friends?
3. Important dates (This listing will help you in later writing the case statement and other publicity). Dates of organization and anniversary. Erection of buildings. Previous fund raising events and successes. Inauguration of outstanding presidents or faculty.
4. Board of governors. List for each member: occupation, years on board, largest single gift, last gift (amount and date), which ones should be interviewed.
5. Needs of the institution. What, if any, are the operating needs? Amounts? What are the capital needs? Itemize, with probable cost, in order of priority.
6. List of major prospects. List individually, with occupation, relationship to institution, largest single gift, last gift (amount and date), estimate of hoped-for gift.
7. Present financial promotion. What types of fund raising are held? Who is responsible? How often conducted? Are volunteers used?
8. Accreditation. What agencies? When?
9. Enrollment full-time. List number of students per year for the past decade.
10. Description of buildings. Age? Size? Condition?
11. Office records. What types of materials are in files? What condition are they in? What giving records are there?
12. Former campaigns. List each drive by dates, purposes, goals, pledges received, cash received. State total number of gifts and catalog by number and amount of gifts at various dollar levels. Give costs and geographical spread of each campaign.
13. Sets of financial figures for last year, for five years ago, and for ten years ago:
    A. Assets. Itemize by current funds, loan funds, annuity funds, plant funds, endowment.
    B. Liabilities. Itemize by same groupings as for Assets.
    C. Income. Itemize by educational, auxiliary, noneducational, deficit (surplus).
    D. Expenses. Itemize by same groupings as for Income.
14. Ten year record of bequests. List by years. State whether from alumni or others.

15. Ten year record of annual fund receipts. List by years. Give number of gifts, as well as amounts.
16. Ten year record of gifts other than annual fund or bequests. List by year and number of gifts.
17. Forms to be used in the external (interviewing) phase. Make a separate sheet for each interview. List the nine questions given, with space for answers to each. List personal impressions of the interviewer.

THE EXTERNAL ASPECT
OF THE FEASIBILITY STUDY

The purpose of the interviews is to obtain a cross-section attitude of your influential supporters. Seek out both those capable of large donations and those who are leaders in influencing others. If the size of your clientele and your goal warrant, interview at least fifty persons. Larger goals, especially in nationwide efforts, require many more. In the denominational campaign of the United Church of Christ to raise, from 6,600 congregations, funds for higher education for minorities, we held fifty-five meetings in thirty-five states, asking uniform questions in each. At the close of each session, a total of 1,742 persons filled out our survey questionnaires.

The interviewing is not so much attempting to discover *if* the institution can raise funds as it is to discover *how* and *how much* and *when*. The survey for the YWCA of Harford revealed that the community would not support an immediate drive, but that if the YW allowed the YMCA to campaign first (they were better prepared), and, meanwhile, explored certain cooperative ventures with the YM, there would be support. Three years later the campaign was held, raising well over $2 million, making possible a new eight-story building.

There are five requirements for the external feasibility study. The first is a good list of potential interviewees. Someone needs to find out the true attitudes of your most influential public before you seek funds, especially if you are seeking large capital gifts. You must seek out those persons who will be expected to give in the larger amounts or those able to influence others who may give significantly. Among this group, of course, will be a number of trustees and a few administrators. Young persons and other persons of very limited means or influence will be of no help at this point.

The second requirement concerns the person who conducts the interviews, and the one who writes the report. It is best when the study is made by an outsider, who is better able to see the problem as a whole, who can stand where the public stands and view the scene dispassionately. Someone who is able to ask further questions when dissatisfaction is voiced. The interviewer who only records what he or she wants to hear is doing your institution no good.

It is preferable to have a seasoned interviewer do the study. This person knows what attitudes and responses to look for, and is attuned to nuances that may lead to partial success—or to failure. Most feasibility studies are done by professional fund raisers. Above all, the interviewer must keep the opinion-gathering confidential. This is requirement three. The interviewer must assure the one being queried that his or her name will not be used in any way. This person must guard the records of his or her conversations so that they do not fall into the hands of administrators. At the conclusion of one survey the chief administrator asked for my interview cards. I had to refuse. Otherwise I would have broken faith with fifty or more persons.

The surveyor must ask the right questions. Requirement four. The true sentiments of those interviewed—the feelings which indicate whether one will support a drive by time and money—is brought out through a series of select questions. These questions revolve around nine points:

1. What is the interviewee's attitude toward the institution? If there is criticism, how significant?
2. What constructive suggestions are made?
3. What does he or she think of staff and administration?
4. Is the interviewee acquainted with the needs of the institution?
5. What is there about the institution which particularly attracts the interviewee?
6. Does the interviewee believe the institution has a good case? Is the campaign a good idea?
7. Will the interviewee be willing to give? The question of how much is not asked.
8. Will he or she give time to the drive?
9. Is there any reason why the campaign should not be held at once?

It is the answer to these nine points that determine whether a campaign should take place and when. These questions are not so much asked directly as brought out in conversation. In addition, the surveyor needs to record his or her own impressions of each call. What size gift might the prospect make? Would the prospect be apt to accept a position of leadership? Where would the interviewer classify him or her, ranging from enthusiastic to opposed?

Of all the preceding questions, there are four basic ones which can be measured as norms for probable success, all things being equal. These four are:

- FIRST—Does the interviewee have confidence in your institution? How much? Or why not?
- SECOND—Does he or she believe in the fund-raising objectives as proposed?
  What parts particularly appeal? What changes might he or she suggest?
- THIRD—Will he or she be willing to work in the drive?
- FOURTH—Will he or she be willing at a later date to make a gift?

Your institution may have an additional question or two to add, but answers to these four questions will give you guidance in determining when to campaign, for what to seek funds, and what your goal should be.

The fifth requirement is the weighing of answers to the four questions asked. Time and again I have found heads of organizations blinded by proximity to the appeal of their cause and thus unable to think of realistic dollar goals. Often this attitude is true of the inner group of advisors—six or eight in number. Hence it is essential to survey the attitude of potential givers who are not charmed by the snake eyes of self-delusion.

Interviewing such a large group means no institution or society can get 100 percent approval. Should this occur, it would mean that the organization was not daring enough, was guilty of a milk-toast program.

A positive response to a careful feasibility study would call for:

- 80 percent approval to question one
- 80 percent approval to question two
- 60 percent approval to question three
- 75 percent approval to question four.

What if the responses are not as high as these percentages? Then reconsideration must be given to the entire campaign. If the gap is not too great, maybe the goal needs to be lowered. Or the opening delayed for several months. If the gap is markedly lower than the percentages desired, the campaign may need to be postponed or even shelved permanently.

CHAPTER 9

Step Two:

Budgeting

*Careful budgeting, which involves forethought to all compo-
nents of the campaign, will save dollars and help to ensure
a proper balance to the spending for different phases of the
drive.*

How much should a campaign or ongoing drive cost? That depends
on such factors as:

– number of prospects.
– how you will reach these prospects. Is it all to be by direct mail, by
  visitation, or how? Direct mail campaigns can cost 50 percent or more
  of receipts.
– the appeal of your cause. Is it readily apparent, or must you spend
  much effort in getting the public to understand?
– is your appeal to go only to club or organization members, or to
  the entire community, or to certain persons statewise, or is it to be
  nationwide or even international?

Some institutions—those with seasoned staffs, well-organized
offices, easily defined constituencies, and good track records of fund
raising—can raise capital funds for as little as 3 percent. On the
other hand, some college annual funds cost as much as 35 percent
to maintain. We suggest, open to many individual differences, that
a rule of thumb be 10 percent of the goal. Depending on geographical spread, size and experience of the institution, and most impor-

tantly, size of the top six or ten gifts, costs may vary from 5 percent to 20 percent.

In 1968 a study of twenty-seven capital campaigns among independent secondary schools in America, with goals ranging from $200,000 to $4 million, raised $27 million at an average cost of 4.4 percent, reports the New York City firm of Marts and Lundy.

The American Cancer Society states that its fundraising costs are 11.7 percent.

The Ohio Baptist Churches raised $1 million for a special cause from 325 congregations at a cost of $100,000. This included full-time professional counsel. Other denominations or bodies which are willing to accept quotas (not so the Baptists!) can raise their money for less cost.

A survey of capital drives among hospitals reveals these costs, all including the fixed fee (which is not a percentage of amount raised). Professional direction was given by Haney Associates of Concord, Massachusetts:

	Raised	Cost
Community Hospital, Troy, Pa.	$500,800	7.46%
Memorial Hospital, Union City, Pa.	$528,276	8.58%
Community Health Center, Hillsdale, Mich.	$970,000	5.68%
Floyd Valley Hospital, Le Mars, Ia.	$1,463,000	2.78%
St. Olaf Hospital, Austin, Minn.	$1,881,036	2.62%
Desert Hospital, Palm Springs, Ca.	$6,000,000	3.79%

Bear in mind that costs of a large capital campaign are less when annual funds have been maintained. This is so because staffs are trained, prospect lists are in good shape, cultivation has been continuous, and a source of volunteer workers' names is at hand.

Likewise, a successful capital campaign makes the annual enlistment easier and therefore cheaper.

The main items of a fund-raising budget are:

1. Preliminary feasibility study.
2. Salaries.
   Staff director. This item could range from zero for all donated time to 100 percent of salary of one or more staff persons.
   Secretarial. An absolute must.
3. Office expenses.
4. Office rent. Sometimes a building owner will give free rent in lieu of a donation.

5. Promotion, postage, printing, photography.
6. Mailing house charges, if used.
7. Travel and lodging, if any.
8. Campaign meals, if any. Campaign meals really pay for themselves. It is essential that volunteers get together from time to time. Mealtime is often the easiest way to work this out.
9. Fund counsel fee, if any.

There are pros and cons to professional fund-raising fees. The quality of individual fund raisers varies, as does the quality of doctors and lawyers, but, by and large, the pro raises more dollars than the amateur. Thus he or she tends to become a good investment. But there are other things he or she does, too. The fund raiser can, and should, create a better public relations stance, thus raising the level of willingness to participate for years to come. A few months ago my own minister came to me about a small drive for our little church. "Would I be chairman?" "No, because the congregation would look upon me as one of themselves and thus tend not to follow my advice." "Would I serve on the committee?" "Yes." That was six months ahead of the kick-off. Later he said: "We must pay for some outside professional help, for I have been unable to get our chairperson to move." Many organizations run into the same problem.

CHAPTER 10

Step Three:
Scheduling

Unless one plans ahead, the early phases of a drive will take too much time, resulting in either an expensive prolongation of the campaign or a crimping of the closing phases. Without a calendar it is almost impossible to divide duties among staff or volunteers. A detailed calendar, adjusted as time goes on, enables you to set deadlines, to reserve dates and meeting places, and to check on progress.

We usually make several calendars in a drive. We begin with a sketchy schedule for the entire period (whether it be six weeks or six years). Soon we need to revise and add. Then we revise several times; we may have eight or ten calendars before we finish. But the important thing is that we must always plan ahead—as far ahead as possible—and we must see it in writing.

In directing a campaign for Union College we desired to hold a banquet in New York City for all alumni. This would require a room seating 1,000 or more at tables. Now even New York City has trouble providing a good meal in an attractive setting for 1,000 persons. Only the Waldorf-Astoria Hotel could handle that size. But our first several choices of dates were not available. So we finally had to revise our entire spring calendar since our drive was dependent upon this opening event.

In setting up an eight month schedule for a theological seminary (Pacific School of Religion, Berkeley, California) to raise funds to finish paying for a soon-to-be-erected building, the original calendar was divided into two phases—meetings and publicity:

A. Meetings

October —complete pledging by each member of the board. (You need to be able to tell the public: "Every trustee of our organization has already given.")
—name the campaign general committee
—name the campaign steering committee; that is, the executive group of the campaign committee
—name the major gift committee

November —conduct a drive among the faculty
—begin semimonthly meetings of steering committee
—schedule frequent meetings of major gift committee
—launch major gift drive
—set up a pilot program in one or two local churches to solicit some individual pledges

December —schedule meetings of steering committee
—continue major gift drive
—plan future local church drives
—cease active campaigning between December 15 and New Year's

January —clean up major gift solicitation
—schedule meeting of general committee
—schedule meetings of steering committee
—launch local church drives

February–May
—continue series of local church drives

May —plan mail solicitation of all not called upon

B. Publicity

September—get photographs
—engage writer

October —writing and printing of campaign brochure (Statement of Case)

November —distribution of brochure
—Newsletter #1

January —Newsletter #2
February —Newsletter #3
March —Newsletter #4
April —Newsletter #5

This schedule, while covering the salient features of a campaign, did not allow sufficient time for organization and cultivation. The problem was twofold: (1) the seminary covered a five-state area, and thus additional time was needed to reach first the trustees and second the interested local congregations. (2) the seminary was without a president. Many persons, including a number of trustees, would not pledge significant amounts until a president was named. Since a president was not secured until the eight month period ended, the schedule experienced major postponements.

Here is what happened.

1. Professional counsel arrived, August, 1977. Goal: $1,750,000. (There was a gift of one million dollars from a foundation.)
2. The trustees took four months to complete pledging (instead of one month).
3. The faculty pledging was completed on time.
4. The major gift committee needed six months to organize and conduct a very limited drive in the late spring.
5. Because of the delay in securing gifts, only one newsletter was distributed.
6. No church was willing to conduct a drive before the president was secured.
7. June, 1978—$1,295,000 raised. Counsel in final report recommended enlarging staff.
8. July, 1978—goal increased to $2 million. Staff increased threefold.
9. Development budget raised in two years from $56,000 to $79,000, plus a supplement of $40,000 from a foundation, given specifically to strengthening fund raising.
10. December, 1978—new president named. $1,710,000 raised.
11. December, 1979—$2,129,000. Campaign closed.
12. February, 1980—new building dedicated.

Note: None of the preceding figures include gifts from annual funds, bequests, or other special gifts. The trustees announced that 1978-1979 "was one of the most successful years for gift income in the school's history."

The drawing up of a calendar did not compensate for the unwillingness of the constituency to pledge when there was no president. It did, however, outline the steps to be followed, which were subsequently taken successfully.

The campaign for a new Science-Arts building for Kingswood School in West Hartford Connecticut, moved much closer to its original schedule. The solicitation was organized into five phases, determined by size of the contemplated gift. In other words, five different groups of workers were engaged in their own effort, resulting in five small campaigns correlated in one drive requiring ten months. Form 10–1 is the original schedule worked out for a three month period of one of these five categories—the special gift phase. Form 10–2 is an eleven week calendar of recruiting, training, and solicitation of special and general workers.

The basic rules in setting up a campaign calendar are:

1. Begin with a sketchy outline—on one sheet of paper—of your entire period. This period may be one month or three years.
2. Work backwards. The first date to put down is the conclusion— the final day—of your drive. Continue working backwards, down to the present, putting in only your major events or deadlines.
3. Your first calendar is usually too long a period. You then compress and eliminate items until your schedule fits the time available.
4. From one sketchy calendar, covering your entire period, you then begin working out detailed calendars of shorter periods. If your time available is, for instance, four months, work out four monthly calendars.
5. Spend as much time as needed in refining and detailing your calendar for your first month. Then, revise each month's schedule a week or so before the month opens, repeating steps that have not been completed as originally scheduled and eliminating steps (or dates) that are no longer essential.
6. Show your calendar to all concerned, for suggestions and revisions. It is especially important that you receive the approval of your writer and printer.

Form 10–3 is a five-week calendar used in a church. This can be readily adapted to a club or an organization all of whose prospective givers are concentrated within ten or so square miles. The span of five or six weeks is sufficient provided:

– number of prospect homes do not exceed 300
– all are within ten or less square miles
– top leadership for the drive is available and willing
– all decisions concerning need for funds, setup of office, number of volunteers needed, and agreement on procedure are made *prior* to the opening of the drive.
– you have some professional assistance, even if only part-time

Form 10–1

KINGSWOOD NOW

General Chairman ___James B. Lyon___
　　　　　　　　　BUSINESS ADDRESS　　　PHONE　　　HOME ADDRESS　　　PHONE

Special Gifts Co-Chairman ___Richard E. Dunne, Jr.___
　　　　　　　　　　　　　BUSINESS ADDRESS　　　PHONE　　　HOME ADDRESS　　　PHONE

Special Gifts Co-Chairman ___Charles H. Stamm___
　　　　　　　　　　　　　BUSINESS ADDRESS　　　PHONE　　　HOME ADDRESS　　　PHONE

S.G. = Special Gift

	SUNDAY	MONDAY	TUESDAY	WEDNESDAY	THURSDAY	FRIDAY	SATURDAY
NOV. WEEK 1	9					14 Deadline: Secure 6 S.G. Division Leaders	
WEEK 2	16		18 4:00 P.M. Meeting of 6 S.G. Division Leaders				
WEEK 3	23			26 Deadline: Secure 24 S.G. Captains	Thanks-giving		
WEEK 4	30	1 4:00 P.M. Meeting of 24 S.G. Captains					
DEC. WEEK 5	7					12 Deadline: Secure 96 S.G. Workers	
				DECEMBER			
				JANUARY			
JAN.	11			14 Workers' Instruc-tion Meeting	15 Make-up Meeting		
	18		20	21		23 Begin Solicitation	
			OPENING DINNER (Choose one evening)				

47

ILLUSTRATIVE CAMPAIGN CALENDAR

SG = special gift   GG = general gift

Monday	Tuesday	Wednesday	Thursday	Friday
MARCH 25	26	27	28 Meet with SG Chairman	
APRIL 1	2 Meet with GG Chairman	3	4 Meet with SG Division Leaders and Captains	5
8	9	10 Meet with GG 10 Division Leaders	11	12 Issue First Reporter
15 Deadline: SG Committee Workers enlisted	16	17 Meet with GG Captains	18 SG Training Meeting	19
22	23 SG DINNER Mail brochure	24 SG Solicitation starts	25	26
29	30 SG First Report	MAY 1	2 GG Training Meeting	3 Issue Second Reporter
MAY 6 SG Second Report	7 GG DINNER Mail brochure	8 GG Solicitation starts	9	10
13	14	15 GG First Report	16	17
20	21 GG Second Report	22	23	24 Issue Third Reporter
27	28	29 GG Third Report	30 Holiday	31
JUNE 3	4 GG Fourth Report	5	6	7

Form 10–3

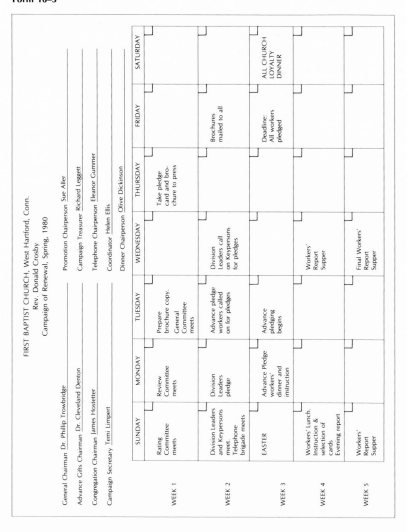

FIRST BAPTIST CHURCH, West Hartford, Conn.
Rev. Donald Crosby
Campaign of Renewal, Spring, 1980

General Chairman Dr. Phillip Trowbridge   Promotion Chairperson Sue Aller

Advance Gifts Chairman Dr. Cleveland Denton   Campaign Treasurer Richard Leggett

Congregation Chairman James Hostetter   Telephone Chairperson Eleanor Gummer

Campaign Secretary Terri Limpert   Coordinator Helen Ellis

    Dinner Chairperson Olive Dickinson

	SUNDAY	MONDAY	TUESDAY	WEDNESDAY	THURSDAY	FRIDAY	SATURDAY
WEEK 1	Rating Committee meets	Review Committee meets	Prepare brochure copy. General Committee meets		Take pledge card and brochure to press		
WEEK 2	Division Leaders and Keypersons meet. Telephone brigade meets	Division Leaders pledge	Advance pledge workers called on for pledges	Division Leaders call on Keypersons for pledges		Brochures mailed to all	
WEEK 3	EASTER	Advance Pledge workers' dinner and instruction	Advance pledging begins			Deadline: All workers pledged	ALL CHURCH LOYALTY DINNER
WEEK 4	Workers' Lunch. Instruction & selection of cards Evening report			Workers' Report Supper			
WEEK 5	Workers' Report Supper			Final Workers' Report Supper			

Extension of any of these factors requires extra weeks. Thus a campaign to get into 1,000 homes may require ten weeks. Should your constituency of 1,000 cover a major metropolitan area, you would need three months or more. Without any professional (or much experienced) counsel, you should extend the times outlined in Form 10–3.

The factors that usually call for the most time are:

- preparation of the case (why you need funds). To be completed *before* the active campaigning begins.
- writing and printing of the brochure setting forth your case.
- securing volunteer callers. Allow a minimum of one week to secure division leaders (see Chapter Eighteen), another week to recruit key persons, and at least two weeks to secure the bottom tier of workers. Even this schedule will call for much push from the top.

Remember, the drawing up of your calendar is the preliminary essential to any financial drive. I find that any short campaign, say six or eight weeks, is greatly simplified once I see all my crucial dates on a sheet of paper before me.

CHAPTER **11**

Step Four:
Preparing the case

*If there be one step that is most damaging to any campaign,
it is the too hasty preparation of the case for raising funds.
If the institution has not carefully thought through the "why"
of the drive, the constituency will not be persuaded to participate wholeheartedly.*

What is the purpose of your organization—your school? How easily
can you state it? In how few words can you write it down?

Why do you desire to raise funds? What is your financial need?
Are you going for capital needs (building, debt, retirement of mortgage, permanent funds) or for operating funds? What is on your
list of needs that will appeal to the public? In brief, what is your
justification in asking your constituency to give?

Before going to the public, each organization must think
through the rationale for the appeal and reduce it to writing. Preferably on one sheet of paper.

Sounds simple. But for many groups it is complicated indeed.
Fuzziness in this task will set the stage for failure in your drive.
The mere fact that you, and your board, desire dollars will not lead
to a public response, no matter how well organized your effort.
One college in America, desiring funds but not quite sure how to
use these funds, prepared itself for disaster when the chairperson
of the board, without conferring with anyone, announced to a large
commencement audience that the college was entering a capital

drive for thirty million dollars, a sum far beyond their ability. It took at least a decade for the college to recover from this rash statement.

The preparation of your case often involves long-range planning. You need to analyze what your financial needs are, and, most important, what the answering of those needs will do for your institution over a period of years. You must analyze what will be the position of your organization five—even ten—years from now if the effort succeeds.

People do not like to give to causes or institutions that are floundering. They give, when they do give, not merely to keep your doors open another year, but primarily for what they believe the institution will be accomplishing in the future. Particularly is this true of capital campaigns. This "look at the future" must be clearly set forth in your case statement. And the ultimate aim must be what the new funds will do for people rather than an institution.

The annual appeal differs in that you are directing attention to your aims and goals of the coming year. Yet even here the public is thinking in terms of longer than one year. The only exception is that cause—an election campaign is an example—which has no reason for existence beyond the coming year. Thus your appeal for annual funds is based, not upon the cost of your utility bills and your payroll, but upon your desired program objectives for the next twelve months and beyond. Again, what will you be doing for people in the future?

So even the annual appeal, to be most successful, should be based upon a modified long-range program.

The statement of the case can range from the simple to the most complicated objectives. It is, of course, the more complicated that require the clearest setting forth of the facts. Even the paying off of a mortgage ahead of time can become involved. The Covenant Presbyterian Church of Fort Myers, Florida, decided to have a campaign to prepay their mortgage (not due in full for eleven years), and here is what their case statement included:

1. Present balance of mortgage		$303,327
2. Total cost if not paid before 1991		486,350
3. Savings if paid immediately		183,022
4. Savings if paid in full in about two years time	from	$120,000
	to	140,000
5. Additional available funds made possible by setting a goal higher than amount needed for mortgage	from	$130,000
	to	180,000

6. Present mortgage payment schedule
of $3,550 per month (now in current
operating budget) would be eliminated
before the three year pledge period
ends. Therefore, additional funds for
new programming would be available from
the liquidation of this item.

The compiling of these figures required several weeks of thought by a committee of church leaders. Even then their case was not complete. For some business people believed that it was not wise to pay off a 9 percent mortgage when current mortgage rates were close to 15 percent. The church needed to state that congregations, unlike individuals or corporations, did not receive any tax benefits from interest payments. Interest payments were pure costs without any benefits to the church. Bob Rockwell, campaign chairman, set forth this concept by a simple phrase: "0% is better than 9%."

A small organization may be able to state its case in a printed half page or less. An older, more established institution, desiring several million dollars, may require several printed pages. But whether short or long, the statement must be so clear that "he who runs may read."

HOW TO GO ABOUT PREPARING THE CASE

The appeal for public support must be founded upon the philosophy of the institution—must jibe with the innermost essence of your organization.

The statement of the case in a capital campaign calls for long-range planning. Where does the institution intend to be in ten years? How will capital funds today help? The first step is to name a committee to study long-range objectives, to establish a broad, idealistic foundation. Top leadership from administration and trustees must be in this group.

The case must set forth humanitarian concerns. What will it do for people, for the individual? We repeat: people give to people for people. What social or artistic problems will the new funds help to solve? How can problems be turned into opportunities?

The case must state the competence of your group to handle the problem and to disburse the money for such purpose. Hence a second step is an analysis of your stewardship of funds in the past as well as your future financial plans.

A third step is the outlining of a plan of procedure. What is your organizational setup? What is your timing? Who will give leadership? Is there a priority in the spending of new funds? Where are the funds expected to come from? What size and type of gifts are being sought?

Next, there will be required a spelling out of how the funds will be used. What are the items involved? How much will each cost? Who will supervise the disbursements, whether it be for a new building, major renovations, debt reduction, new salaries, or what?

Finally, the statement of the case must be put into readable form. This need not be an expensive brochure of four colors, high gloss stock, and lavish layout. In fact, such a presentation sometimes works against you. Think of your readers as being intelligent, concerned citizens who want to help improve society. More and more case statements are now being neatly typed, offset, and placed in simple binders. Your very lack of anything smacking of extravagance and high pressure will work in your favor.

CHAPTER **12**

Step Five:

Setting the goal

A goal set too high is readily perceived by the public and results in fewer dollars being raised than if the goal were realistic. A goal set too low results in self-reproach of the administrators. There is a method of arriving at an attainable goal.

Every drive for funds needs a goal—a dollar objective. It is a serious mistake to say: "We are going for all we can get." The public will not take such a drive seriously.

If your institution is preparing for an annual drive, and has had several years experience in raising such money, your goal will be based upon the results of the last three years. Use an average of three years, since sometimes the last year was disastrous, or at least unusual. There should be an increase in requests, of course, since an institution that stands still is an institution that is dying. But the increase must be justified in your publicity. How much increase do you desire? What for?

The higher the increase you seek, the clearer must be your rationale. A large increase, more than 10 percent above previous efforts, can be accomplished only if one or more of the following is true:

— the need is dramatically evident. Such, for instance, would be the American Red Cross appealing for funds to relieve victims of a recent widespread flood.

– the future opportunities are both evident and clearly set forth.
– the organization of the drive has been completely revised, such as a new administration, or the use of many new volunteers, or the employment of professional counsel.

The setting of a goal for a capital campaign is a more complicated procedure. Yet even here the experience of preceding capital campaigns is a guide. Most such drives can set goals higher than received in former campaigns. This is so because of inflation and increased personal incomes, because of longer experience in fund raising, and because, in cases of successful past efforts, of a greater awareness of the public of what you are accomplishing.

The goal for a capital campaign is based upon three factors:

– the need for funds, clearly and convincingly set forth in the case statement. Have these needs been translated into opportunities?
– the public appreciation of what the organization has accomplished and belief that it will continue to serve in a worthy manner.
– the organization of the campaign. Is the timing appropriate, bearing in mind that "it is always the wrong time to raise money"? Is the planned organization sufficient to do the job? Who is heading the drive? Do you have professional fund raising counsel?

The friends of an institution seem to have an innate sense of what size goal might be attained. By "friends" we do not mean only the administration, since their objectivity is clouded by their own sense of mission. Administrators tend to be overly optimistic. Nor can the board of trustees properly set the goal, for the same reason.

How, then, does your organization determine the innate sense of your constituency?

By asking them.

Asking many persons, especially influential leaders, persons of sound business judgment. These persons, of course, need to be given a sketch of the future planning of the institution, of what will be done if funds are raised.

Three or four persons may be too high or too low in their estimates. Therefore, you should sound out a larger group. If your institution has an operating budget of $100,000 or more, you might interview twenty persons. If your budget is a half million, try to interview forty or fifty. If you are at a level in excess of a million dollars, or if you work in several states, you may need to interview several hundred. You then can deal with average responses.

The interviewing concerning the size of your goal is most effective when done by an outsider, one who does not have a vested interest, who can be completely objective.

Details of this procedure are set forth in Chapter Eight.

There is another type of interviewing, done in a group session. It is highly effective if the right persons are in the room. By right persons we mean persons of influence, community leaders, especially business leaders. This gathering is often called a consultation meeting, since it is a group called together to consult with you in setting a goal.

When one college was ready to launch a drive in its hometown, we invited ten business leaders—bankers, industrialists, lawyers, and prominent alumni to serve as the consultation group on setting a goal. The president of the college and the chairperson of the campaign were present. Around the luncheon table we told of our need and our plans for a national campaign. We put before the group three sets of "Scale of Gifts Needed" for goals of $1 million, $1.5 million, and $2 million. After frank discussion the group agreed, and the college accepted, a local city goal of $1 million. Form 12–1 sets forth the goal, with its breakdown of gifts required, that the group decided upon. Part way through the drive we issued Form 12–2 as a report of progress. Three months later the hometown drive reached $1,005,389, in addition to city gifts previously donated of $715,000.

Form 12–1
A COLLEGE HOMETOWN CAMPAIGN

SCALE OF GIFTS NEEDED
for a goal of $1,000,000

No.	In the range of	Total
1	$100,000	$100,000
2	50,000	100,000
4	25,000	100,000
5	20,000	100,000
7	15,000	105,000
8	10,000	80,000
18	5,000	90,000
30	3,000	90,000
85	1,000	85,000
160		$850,000
Many of less than 1,000		150,000
		$1,000,000

A most valuable tool in capital fund raising—and now increasingly used in annual funds—is the "scale of gifts needed." This analysis is used three ways: first, as a guide preliminary to setting a goal; second, as a guide to larger gift prospects; and third, as an oft-repeated portion of the reports to workers during the course of campaigning.

Form 12–2
A COLLEGE HOMETOWN CAMPAIGN

SCALE OF GIFTS NEEDED AND THOSE RECEIVED TO DATE
(Sample of report issued midway through campaign)

Number needed	In the range of	Total	Number received	Total
1	$100,000	$100,000		$
2	50,000	100,000	1	50,194
4	25,000	100,000	1	25,000
5	20,000	100,000		
7	15,000	105,000	2	30,000
8	10,000	80,000	6	60,000
18	5,000	90,000	8	49,500
30	3,000	90,000	7	27,000
85	1,000	85,000	75	93,839
160		850,000	100	335,533
Many of less than 1,000		150,000	481	127,265
Previous City Gifts				200,000
GRAND TOTAL		$1,000,000	581	$662,798

Form 12–3 gives the scale of gifts needed, and final results, for a small college and a large university in their capital campaigns.

Form 12–3

SCALE OF GIVING FOR A SMALL COLLEGE AND A LARGE UNIVERSITY

A SMALL MIDWEST COLLEGE: GOAL $2,162,000

Number of gifts needed	Number of gifts received	In the range of	Total needed	Total received	%
1	—	$300,000	$300,000	—	
1	1	150,000	150,000	$155,000 ⎫	25%
1	4	100,000	100,000	419,910 ⎭	
2	3	75,000	150,000	242,850 ⎫	
4	4	50,000	200,000	214,456 ⎬	32%
10	10	25,000	250,000	268,974 ⎭	
15	8	15,000	225,000	133,855 ⎫	
20	17	10,000	200,000	197,311 ⎪	
35	33	5,000	175,000	189,104 ⎬	33%
45	31	3,000	135,000	103,892 ⎪	
77	100	1,000	77,000	139,326 ⎭	
211	211		$1,962,000	$2,064,678	
	1,604	Under $1,000	200,000	218,761	10%
TOTAL	1,815		$2,162,000	$2,283,439	

A LARGE UNIVERSITY PROGRAM: GOAL $100,000,000

Number of gifts needed	Number of gifts received	In the range of	Total needed	Total received	%
12–15	12	Over $1,000,000	$18,000,000	$24,800,000	28%
125–160	142	$100,000—1,000,000	31,000,000	38,500,000	44%
550–660	623	10,000—100,000	15,000,000	17,900,000	20%
—	—	Under 10,000	11,000,000	6,800,000	8%
			75,000,000	88,000,000	
		A Foundation	25,000,000	25,000,000	
			100,000,000	113,000,000	

CHAPTER 13

Step Six:
Compiling lists

*Funds cannot be raised without asking. Whom do you ask?
How large is your list of potential donors? How does an organization build up its list? There are tested ways.*

Suppose you have few—or no—names on your prospect list.

You should not rely solely on a grant from government or from one or two foundations or one corporation. If you are in a position to realize much of your financial needs from such a source—fine. But few new organizations can.

You must beware, if your society has had no experience in raising funds, of thinking all you need is to present your case to some foundation or to some state or federal agency. Some organizations are, assuredly, financed in large part by grants from one or two of these sources. But there is usually some special reason, such as a board member having an inside track to a foundation or corporation, or having some unique objective which has fit some niche of a governmental agency, presented at exactly the right moment. Most grants are awarded to well-established institutions.

There simply are not sufficient funds available through foundations or governmental agencies to meet more than a modicum of needs presented to them. Thus we strongly advise that you think of these large grant-giving units as but one arrow in your quiver.

The great majority of gift-seeking institutions must first establish a track record before being able to tap these sources.

Where, then, do you turn for help? Why, to individuals primarily.

COMPILING A PROSPECT LIST FOR A NEW ORGANIZATION

First prepare some blank lists. Something very simple, such as 8½ x 11 sheets with several columns:

name, address, occupation, business title, source of name, and (sometimes) estimated giving ability

A little pump-priming helps. If you begin by listing twenty or so names, these will help stimulate thinking.

Now go to your trustees and staff. Ask each to give you at least ten names. Tell them not to delay because of lack of addresses. You can get that later.

Now go to influential leaders in your community—secretary of chamber of commerce, bank presidents, trust officers, lawyers, stockbrokers, club secretaries, clergymen. Tell them what you are doing. Even if some give you no names, it is good to get your story across in person to these leaders.

You cannot do this by mail or telephone. It calls for your appearance in person to these people and obtaining names while you are seated or standing in front of them. When you obtain names without addresses, do not spurn them. Do not trust your memory. Write down every name mentioned in conversation. You can tell a fund raiser by two signs: he or (she) always has a pencil and pad handy; the fund raiser does not have a sheen on the seat of his or her clothing, caused by too much time spent at the desk.

You must get out onto the road. You must ask many influential people. Back at your desk, check spellings and obtain addresses by means of telephone books, social registers, Dun and Bradstreet's Million Dollar Directory, printed lists of doctors, lawyers, etc. Your public librarian can be of great help here.

And for gosh sakes, spell those names correctly.

As you begin your mailings, always ask your readers to send in four or five names of acquaintances. Be sure to request that they PRINT names and addresses, with zip codes.

STRENGTHENING THE
PROSPECT LIST OF AN
ESTABLISHED ORGANIZATION

In two campaigns I directed, the prospect list of past donors was dug out of dusty closets, beneath a pile of old records and junk. Not only were these records somewhat out of date, they also revealed giving patterns that, because of the small size of these gifts, were not clear indicators of what we might expect. Nevertheless, there were names of past donors, and upon these skimpy foundations we would begin.

When the YWCA in Hartford, Connecticut, in 1970 found it necessary to build a completely new structure (the old building and site having been sold), I directed the board of managers in bringing in new lists of persons who had not previously given but who tended to be civic-minded. Within a week these people brought in membership lists of city and country clubs, women's societies, friends, and names taken from donor lists of other civic or cultural groups in town.

Results? The YW began with a contributors' list of a little more than 100 names. When the board and staff finished bringing in new names, a committee deleted all persons not able to give $100 minimum. That left 2,100 names. These were again rated by a committee which determined there were 1,200 capable of giving a minimum of $1,000. Another meeting was then held to further evaluate this list. See Chapter Fifteen for rating procedure.

Some organizations *think* they have a list when they don't—at least not for fund raising. A small art school in New England had a mailing list of 4,000 names. They had sent an appeal in their newsletter to become a friend of the institution. Despite the offer of 20 percent discount in their supply store to all who contributed $10 (definitely a money-losing proposition), there were only seven responses. Apparently this result catapulted the school into hiring their first development director. The list of 4,000 names was good only for publicity purposes, and since it was a hodgepodge of some alumni (not all), some parents (not all), and many high schools, it was not even a good publicity list. The development director is now giving priority to building a list of possible donors.

You may be thinking about renting or purchasing lists from commercial firms. There are definite pitfalls here. Guidance in this labyrinth is given in the following section by a professional.

Before you can launch an annual direct-mail appeal, you must have a prospect list. How do you build a list for direct mail? When do you purchase, rent, or exchange lists? How do you test lists?

What do you include in your package? To answer these questions, and many more, I have asked Jeanne Brodeur to write the following section.

THE DEMYSTIFICATION
OF DIRECT MAIL

Jeanne Brodeur
Director of Development
WGBH
WGBH Educational Foundation
Boston, Massachusetts

Mention the words "direct mail" to many fund raisers and you create a wall of negative feelings that no other source of contributions creates. The odd thing, of course, is that all of us are involved with direct mail in one way or another. Every time you send a letter of solicitation asking the recipient to respond in some way, you're using direct mail or direct marketing as it is commonly referred to today (to encompass other media such as television, radio and newspapers). Your renewals are as much direct mail as your new donor campaign.

There are four factors that affect every mail solicitation you send. If you'll just keep in mind, in their order of importance, direct mail will become an easy and more effective method of raising funds for you:

- LIST
- PACKAGE
- TIMING
- VISIBILITY

List

Simply put, your first and most important aspect of direct mail is "Whom am I mailing to?" You need to find people who are interested in your service or organization. Unfortunately, you'll find lists the most difficult area to master, especially when your aim is prospecting for new contributors.

A definitive study of lists would require a book of its own, but there are some basic do's and dont's. Keep in mind that the following types of lists are given by priority from high to low.

Your Own Member/Contributor List

Your list as a source of renewals is your most valuable asset. Imagine what it would be like to start from scratch each year. Horrifying! But don't be afraid to ask for additional gifts at other times during the year, especially in December (holiday and end-of-tax-year time) and at the end of your fiscal year (deficit time). Nobody will give like someone who has already given. Be honest and straight-forward and be careful to warn them that this gift is *in addition* to their regular gift.

Your Lapsed/Expired Contributors

I cannot stress enough the critical nature of maintaining a lapsed file. I cringe every time a fund raiser confesses to me that he or she simply deletes and discards names of past members/contributors. There is no way you can buy a more effective and productive list and there it is, free except for clerical costs. You can mail to lapsed members at least four times a year with good results (remember the list is constantly changing). Remember to clean your lapsed list with an ADDRESS CORRECTION REQUESTED at least one time a year. It will pay off in increased response and dollar profits with each mailing.

Donors to Similar Causes

Most often other donor lists are available on an exchange only basis. In return for 5,000 names and addresses of their contributors, you supply 5,000 of yours to them. Don't faint! If you're worried that if another organization solicits your contributors they will no longer give to you, you're dead wrong. Research shows they will continue to respond to your appeals as well, if not better than ever. If you do exchange, never give more names than you can expect to get back immediately. Ask the other organization to sign a letter verifying they will use the list you supply only once and will not copy it or keep a record in any way. You, of course, should do likewise for them.

Become acquainted with directors of development from the other nonprofit groups in your community. Discuss an exchange and deal together on a peer basis. In this way there will be no cost but the running of your names on labels for them. Exchanges can also be arranged through a broker who will normally charge a $5 or $10 per thousand service charge. These exchanges through a broker are mainly for exchanges with national fund raising organizations such as the Epilepsy Foundation or the American Heart Association.

I realize that exchanging lists invariably causes discussion of privacy and ethics. These arguments have been around for years and will be debated for years to come. The fact remains—donor lists you acquire by exchange will respond to your appeals better than any list you rent or compile.

There are many ways you can safeguard your own members. Although it is not required by law, it is recommended that you have a method to code a donor as not-exchangeable. You should notify your donors if you exchange lists and give them the option not to have their name given. Be choosy about whom you exchange with to avoid criticism and ask for a sample mailing piece from the other organization.

Subscription Lists

People who subscribe to magazines, newsletters, and periodicals which cover the same area of interest as your organization are good prospects. For example, if you are soliciting funds for a science museum, or a scientific organization, a likely prospect would be a subscriber to *Science 80* (the magazine of the American Association for the Advancement of Science).

Merchandise and Catalog Sales Lists

If you look for high quality and high cost merchandise catalog lists, you'll find a good source for your message. A solicitation from the National Audubon Society might be sent to a list of buyers from L. L. Bean or Eddie Bauer.

NOTE: all of the lists just mentioned are "mail responsive." By that I mean they have been put on the list because they responded to some offer or solicitation that arrived in the mail. This makes them more likely to respond to a mail appeal from you. Prices for subscriber lists such as *Time* magazine or merchandise/catalog lists such as Carol Wright Mail Order Buyers range from $35 to $50 per thousand names.

Subscription and catalog lists are best procured through a qualified list broker or mail house. When approaching a list broker or mail house ask for a list of clients and call them for references. In many cases it will be to your benefit to deal with a single mail house who will coordinate list purchase, printing and mailing for you. One-stop shopping can save considerable time and trouble for you. Check with other organizations in your area, or if you are a chapter of a national organization, check with your national office or other affiliates. The truth of the matter is that there are very few full-service mail houses (ones that can handle every aspect of your mailing including creative services) around, but you may want to consider using one even if it is many miles away from your community.

Compiled Lists

This covers a very broad area. To highlight a few lists that you would consider to be compiled lists I refer to lists of businesses, dentists, doctors, alumni and many others. Often a compiled list carries a fancy name invented by the compiler to provoke your desire and interest. These lists are primarily compiled from the yellow pages, directories, and organizations' membership lists. Beware of this type of compiled list except for special targeted mailings. Always ask when the last update was done and how often the list is cleaned and updated. Be sure to purchase the list (costs running from $30 to $60 per thousand) from a reputable compiler. Especially beware of locally compiled lists unless you can verify deliverability (be sure that addresses are current). For the small mailer it is often possible to compile your own list from the same sources.

You will also find demographic lists (such as ones maintained by R. H. Donnelley, Metromail and R. L. Polk)* sometimes considered to be compiled lists. These are constructed from telephone books, but the information is fed into a computer and then overlayed with census statistics. Census tracts are then categorized by income, length of residency, age and many other factors.

There are many ways to select the best names for your appeal. However, too many organizations and fund raisers take large areas of a demographic list making no selections, simply because they wish to mail a large quantity. The list itself is far less expensive (generally $15 to $30 per thousand) than those previously mentioned, but it will also be less responsive on the whole. Careful selection can produce increased response results, but the ideal use of a demographic list is to "fill in" to a desired quantity after you have exchanged or rented other lists.

Again, I don't recommend a local demographic list, unless you know it is kept up to date. Also avoid resident or occupant lists which may be even cheaper, but lack any sense of personalization.

You can indeed compile your own prospect list. For many small nonprofit organizations this is a necessity, not a luxury. How? If

---

* R. H. Donnelley, 1301 West 22nd St., Oak Brook, IL 60521
  Metromail, 485 Lexington Avenue, New York, N.Y. 10017
  R. L. Polk, 6400 Monroe Boulevard, Taylor, MI 48180

you are a museum or you get visitor traffic, use a guest book at the reception area and encourage people to sign their names and addresses. Keep lists of people who write to your organization for information. Ask your board members or present donors to suggest likely prospects. There are many other ways if you take the time to review your organization and your prospects. Use directories, annual reports and programs to your advantage.

As you can see, this information on lists is just skimming the surface. Your best bet, if you are in a position to rent lists, is to find a list broker or mail house with heavy *fund-raising experience.* Considerably more difficult than it sounds. List renting involves minimum quantities of 5,000 or more and at $40–$60 per thousand, it's not for everyone. Question list suggestions from the broker or mail house and try where possible to get statistics to prove response to this list from other fund raisers of a similar nature.

The ideal situation would allow you to test various kinds of lists available over the course of several years, but we don't all have that luxury. Whatever you do, keep proper statistics on the performance of every list you use. Not only the percentage of response but the average gift for each list. Check the cost benefit ratio for each list (dollar raised for each dollar spent).

Figure 1. MAILING RESPONSE STATISTICS FROM A PUBLIC TELEVISION MAILING BY LIST

List	% response	Average gift	Cost benefit
Changing Times	1.93	$15.26	1–1.45
Common Cause Actives	4.62	$25.54	1–5.88
Harper's	1.62	$18.65	1–1.49
Southern Living	1.19	$15.72	1– .95
OVERALL MAILING:	2.33	$20.99	1–2.44

Regardless of the source of the list or the size, it is ridiculous to mail without looking at the response. In Figure 1 you see that by deleting the lowest producer the results for follow-up mailings will improve. These valuable statistics are the tools with which you can improve the performance of your direct-mail solicitation. PLEASE NOTE: These results are compiled as illustrations only. Your results may be different.

Code each list and look for this information—number of pieces returned, dollars returned, percentage of return, average gift, cost for pieces mailed and cost benefit ratio.

Package

What will you mail? A good fund raiser never stops asking himself or herself this question. We're always trying to improve the response to a mailing by improving the package as well as the lists. Your first responsibility is to get your letter or message read. Then your biggest challenge is to make your message as personal as possible regardless of the format you use. Basically, quantity and budget will decide the level of personalization (individually typed, computer generated, preprinted letter) you can afford.

I think it's always best to use a theme or teaser line on the outside envelope to catch attention and to encourage the receiver to open and read your package. Don't obscure it on the envelope— make it large and print the teaser in color if possible. You can then use this teaser or the follow-up thought as the lead into your letter.

The personal touch doesn't necessarily mean a computer letter. It simply means that the tone and copy of the letter are conversational. But bringing personalization to the approach may include adding the date and amount of the last gift (for a renewal to a current donor) or mentioning a prospective donor's special interests that are similar to yours. When soliciting cold prospects (not present donors), the real key is to have the letter sound as though it was written to them alone. Write the letter as though you are talking with one person (someone you know), and avoid at all costs the use of clinical or complicated language that you may understand, but your prospect has never heard. Open the letter in the first paragraph with something to grab their attention and interest, keep your paragraphs short and readable, and strive for a warm and friendly atmosphere between you and the prospective donor. Mention a specific level of giving ($10, etc.) at least twice in the body of the letter. Tell the donor exactly what you want him or her to do and when. There is no sense in beating around the bush when this letter is a solicitation for funds. Remember that people will do what you ask them to do, no less and no more.

Always use a P.S. Many times a reader will skip to the P.S. first and the message there will make him or her read the rest of the letter. It may indeed be the only part of the letter that is ever read and should sum up the action you wish them to take.

A word to fund raisers! I'm the first to admit that my own writing skills are not winners in the contest of copywriting. Don't be defensive. Leave the writing of the letter to others who enjoy and excel at writing. You can still sign your name. After all, the goal is the best possible response to your appeal, not a nomination for a Pulitzer prize.

Graphically, there is a great deal you can do to enhance an

appeal. Use two colors on the letter whenever possible, even if it's only the masthead of your letterhead that is another color besides black. Use a bright, warm and eye-catching color. Use photos that visibly express the work of your organization or photos of people who are benefiting from your work. There are also many ways to give an appearance of a personal touch even though the letter may be preprinted. Your signature should be printed in blue, not black. You would be amazed at how many recipients will think you signed the letter personally. Handwrite the P.S. and print it in the same blue color as the signature.

Your reply mechanism should be uncomplicated, easy to fill in, and preaddressed back to you. There is new research that shows it is no longer necessary to pay return postage on either renewals or prospect mailings. Good news in these times of rising costs and something for you to test. Use a bright color ink on white stock or print black on colored paper stock. State several suggested levels of giving, always starting with the highest level ($100, $50, $25) and ending with the lowest. Give the levels names which are appropriate, such as $100 Patron, $50 Supporter, $25 Friend. Begin the inside of your envelope with a positive statement from the donor. ("YES! Here's my tax-deductible check to help the starving orphans in Cambodia.") Be sure to state to whom to make out the check and include a statement about tax deductibility at the bottom of the envelope.

There are many options for additional inserts to the letter and reply envelope or card/envelope. Most commonly you'll find a brochure in many packages which outlines the work of an organization and makes heavy use of photos, lists benefits of membership, or highlights the premiums available for larger levels of giving. It is often effective to add a small additional note which stresses the urgency of your appeal from another donor to your organization or a recipient of help from you. The use of pieces other than a letter should be ordained by how much information you feel the receiver of this package will need to inspire support. Too often, we make our story and our appeal too long. There is such a thing as too much information.

Naturally, I'm not going to end a section on package without urging you to test whenever possible. The rule of thumb is never test more than one single variable at one time. Test your president's signature against the development director's. Test paying return postage against not. Test different approaches to your appeal.

Now's the time to consider how you'll manage your direct-mail effort, what services you will buy and what you will produce and/or coordinate yourself. The situation for each organization is determined by your size, mailing requirements and budget. In many cities you have access to a membership body of nonprofit organizations such as Massachusetts' Metropolitan Cultural Alliance, or to local chapters of national organizations such as the National Society of Fund Raising Executives. At such meetings and gatherings you can solicit help from peers and professionals about the best course for you.

Timing

There are indeed good and bad times to mail during the year when prospecting for new contributors. As you are well aware, the holiday season in November and December is a typically productive time for soliciting funds. The problem, however, is that everyone has joined the bandwagon and your prospective donor is flooded with mail. Summer is a notoriously bad time for prospecting, though this is more true of the northern states than of the south. Climate has a great deal to do with timing your mailing for maximum productivity over the year.

For your renewals, timing is very important. State of the art encourages the first notice to a donor to renew arriving ten months after the last gift (or two months before the anniversary month, whichever way you prefer to look at it). Rule of the trade is at least four notices spaced something like this:

– First notice—10 months after last gift
– Second notice—11½ months after last gift
– Third notice—13 months after last gift
– Fourth notice—15 months after last gift

You'll notice they are spaced approximately six weeks apart to allow for processing and updating. No one likes to get a message to renew when they sent their check weeks ago.

Figure 2. DONOR'S RENEWAL CYCLE

Date of receipt of last gift:	1st notice sent in:	2nd notice sent in:	3rd notice sent in:	4th notice sent in:
January 1980	November 1980	December 1980	February 1981	April 1981
February 1980	December 1980	January 1981	March 1981	May 1981
March 1980	January 1981	February 1981	April 1981	June 1981
April 1980	February 1981	March 1981	May 1981	July 1981
May 1980	March 1981	April 1981	June 1981	August 1981
June 1980	April 1981	May 1981	July 1981	September 1981

CHAPTER 14

Step Seven:

Correcting lists

An out-of-date list results in much waste of time and money. How correct is your list in terms of proper addresses, deaths, and changes of name? Here are suggestions for correcting one's lists.

A list of prospective or current donors filled with incorrect addresses—or having deceased names—does not particularly help a campaign. Yet it is depressing to note that many organizations do not keep their lists up to date with name and address corrections.

A list needs to be corrected after every mailing. At the very least—annually. There are three methods you should be following to keep your lists current.

First, a statement printed on your outside envelopes requesting return, if recipient has moved, and asking for correct address. Print in all capital letters: ADDRESS CORRECTION REQUESTED two line below your address. Your postman will return corrected envelopes for twenty-five cents each. This is especially important for bulk mailings which the post office may discard if undeliverable.

Second, your return envelope should provide space and specifically request correct name and address of donors responding to your appeal. This allows the giver to correct his or her address. Be sure to ask the donor to print. This will prevent errors by your staff unable to read the handwriting.

Third, ask for help from your active members. This is best done with flat lists of names and addresses given out to an assembled group. See Chapter Fifteen. Another way is to publish in your newsletters names of those whose addresses are unknown, requesting new addresses from readers.

Correcting of lists is a tedious, time-consuming procedure which tends to be neglected, unless assigned to one particular person. Unless your lists have many thousands of names, and thus may require daily or weekly revision, it is more efficient to place all changes of address into one file or drawer, and then make all revisions at one time—preferably a rainy Monday. Make sure that all revisions are made in time to correct addresses before your next mailing, or you may spend another twenty-five cents for a post office correction you already have.

And while you are correcting addresses, you may wish to remove names of all $5 donors. The cost to you of such a gift is horrendously expensive. Seldom does a $5 donor increase his or her giving.

Be sure to add zip numbers to your address lists. You can purchase from your post office an official zip code directory which is easy to use and most invaluable.

It is wise, from time to time, to check on your mailings. This applies both to first class and third class mailings. One way is to include in your lists the addresses of yourself and two or three of your office staff, preferably in different zip areas. Then check after each mail. "Did you receive your copy? When?"

Another way was brought home to me by an experience in a campaign in Washington, D.C. I casually mentioned a recent letter to one of my volunteer leaders. He said he had not received it. I then asked three others, of whom two had not received it, though mailed first class. A week later, on another mailing, the same thing occurred. I then reported it to the postal inspector.

Over a period of three weeks the inspector called my office several times, asking such questions as: "How many pieces did you mail? When? How many did not receive it?" And, most important, "Where did those persons live who did not receive it?"

Finally my secretary said: "Aren't you making a big thing of this?"

"No," I replied. "The inspector is after something."

The inspector did not report the findings to us, but we soon read in the papers that an employee from our local post office had been arrested for dumping sacks of mail in the river.

SETTING UP AN ADDRESS SYSTEM

There are several modern ways of keeping address lists.

A wrong way was in a church of 900 members that I was assisting. They kept their lists on gummed labels, on an 8½ x 11 sheet which could be xeroxed, and the copied labels placed by hand onto an envelope. There was no alphabetical order, simply new names were added to another sheet. As long as the church had a crew of retired volunteers willing to come in every Tuesday to prepare the weekly mailing, there was little problem, since time and efficiency were not factors. But once we needed a system, such as preparing pledge cards, making sure there were no duplications, checking for new names and addresses, keeping corrections up to the minute, and separating members from nonmembers, we wasted many precious hours of our paid staff time merely trying to find names.

The right way begins with a card file, arranged alphabetically. For small lists, one set of alphabetical cards may be sufficient. For larger lists with multiple uses, two or more sets in different order may be necessary. One straight alphabetical (so you can always find the record you need); a second by zip code and alphabetical within zip (for mailings using nonprofit bulk postage); and possibly a third by month and year of gift (for sending renewal notices or payment reminders for pledges).

There must be one set of cards for present donors, another for past donors who have not given recently (but as mentioned in the previous chapter are exceptional prospects), and one set for prospects who have never given; or the cards should be tagged by color codes to identify the name as one of these categories.

For mailings where you are unable to retype each name and address cleanly (this depends on your clerical help), consider using a List Production System (LPS). These cards are the size and shape of computer cards, are blue lined for label position, and can be typed on any typewriter. In addition, you can use the blank space on the rest of the card to code or keep contributing information. They are run through a special xerox machine which generates a continuous cheshire (for machine affixing) or pressure sensitive (for hand affixing) label. Check with your local mailing company for the availability of this system in your area.

Of course, the addressograph systems (metal plates which are pressed against an envelope or label) are still alive and well.

In the modern age, however, no one should negate the use of a computer. Most mail houses maintain a computer system that clients can use to keep a name and address system for a nominal charge. Shop around. Perhaps one of your members or donors works for a computer company, or has a computer system within their business that you can inexpensively piggyback on. Ask around and you'll be amazed at how many people have access to computer systems today.

POSTAL REGULATIONS AND PERMITS

There are two specific areas for which permits are required from your post office and about which you should be acquainted. First, a nonprofit bulk rate permit. The fee for this permit on a calendar year (January to December) is $40, plus a *first time fee* of $30 for a number. This allows the nonprofit organization to pay only $.031 (at present, February 1981) instead of $.15 for first class. The only requirements are:

An indicia with your permit number must be printed on the outside envelope. Here is a sample.

```
Non-Profit Org.
U.S. POSTAGE
PAID
Boston, Mass.
Permit No. 0000
```

There must be at least 200 identical pieces to the mailing.

They must be sorted by zip code and bundled by postal regulations (instructions will be given to you by the post office when you obtain your permit).

You must have proof of a 501(c) status with the IRS for the post office.

Check with your local postmaster for further regulations. Second, you may wish to have a Business Reply Mail permit which allows you to receive Business Reply Envelopes from your donors. This permit is also $40 per calendar year. There are two ways by which you may pay for your Business Reply Envelopes (see correct printed format below) as they come back from your local post office. First they will be delivered to you with your mail and you will immediately pay $.25 per envelope to the mail carrier, or you can arrange to pay a $75 accounting fee each year, maintain a balance of money at your post office and have them deduct $.185 per envelope as they are processed. You should figure the number of envelopes you expect to receive during the year and find out if the $75 accounting fee will be paid for by the savings per piece.

You can no longer use the phrase "Your stamp helps" or any similar phrase on the outside of a Business Reply Envelope. Under new postal regulations, any such envelope using a stamp will be

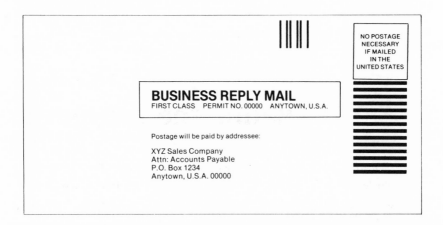

processed as any other piece of Business Reply mail. This means you must collect and tie these envelopes to be returned to your post office for reimbursement of the *postage only.* You will not be reimbursed for the service charge over and above the postage.

Remember to renew your permits every year in November or December to insure no break in service or complications with your post office.

CHAPTER 15

Step Eight:
Rating the prospects

Maximum results can never be reached without rating the possible financial giving of your prospects. Different abilities call for different approaches. Here is how to set up a total goal and how to challenge individual prospects.

WHY RATE?

Every organization seriously thinking of raising funds from the public must determine ahead of time where the greater part of their funds will come from.

This is true of every organization except those which solicit by mail only, asking for a specific amount from each person. Such was *Common Cause,* which was initiated by requesting memberships of $15 each and in 1980 had a membership of 230,000. So are those organizations which raise all of their funds from memberships and have only one class of membership, costing a specified amount.

More and more, however, organizations using direct mail are now offering several classes of membership, each one costing more than the basic type. Thus, you may be invited to become:

– a member—$25
– a sustaining member—$50
– a corporate member—$100
– a lifetime member—$1,000

or, in a capital campaign with three year pledges:

- investor—$1200
- builder— 900
- sustainer—$600
- patron—$300

The preceding illustrations are from organizations which usually have tremendous prospect lists, and often have never categorized the giving ability of their prospects. This system works, if your cause is appealing and your prospect list is enormous.

But what of that society or group or institution which:

- has a list greatly limited by geography or local interest, such as a chamber of commerce
- or, expects to raise most or all of its funds from its own membership, such as a fraternity, church or a temple
- and, especially, that organization which is desirous of raising capital funds.

These organizations must rate their lists. There are several reasons for doing so:

1. to set a reasonable—an attainable—goal
2. to determine who the major givers are apt to be
3. to arrive at a suggested figure for each prospective major giver.

The prospects for larger gifts in a campaign must be determined ahead of time, so that the institution can devote greater attention to this smaller group, provide special publicity pieces or events, and see that proper workers make the call.

It is also essential to have a dollar figure to suggest to your major givers.

About 1960 the Community Chest of Newton, Massachusetts, asked me for help. It was quickly evident that although the directors had asked for general help such as training their solicitors, they needed more basic assistance since their lists had never been evaluated. I readily recognized names on their lists who were being asked to continue their past giving of $15 or $25, persons capable of giving much more. We then set about rating the lists, which resulted in much higher requests—and much higher responses. The drive went well over the top, and I was asked to help again the next year. When it was over, the director stated that my suggestion of rating the lists was alone worth my fee.

Another reason for rating is to set a reasonable goal. This goal setting ahead of time is imperative, for without it the public tends not to take the drive seriously. It is a gross error to state: "We shall raise as much money as we can." Such thinking reveals sloppy preparation—or a lack of thinking. For it shows that the board or administration has not analyzed their needs so that an uninformed public may become informed. In other words, the organization has not done its homework.

A goal can be, and all too often is, set too high. The public seems to have a sense of a goal being unrealistically high. When this happens, the campaign raises less funds than possible, since individual donors feel: "The goal will not be reached anyway. Hence I shall not stretch myself in my giving." A goal should be set so that it can be reached with much work and with top quality leadership.

On the other hand, a goal can be set too low. How disappointing it is to a group who have given hundreds of hours of service to realize at the end that they might have raised a good deal more if their objective had been loftier.

BASIC RULES IN GOAL SETTING

First, some "don'ts" in goal setting.

1. A goal is not set by the architect, contractor, or the bank. Their figures may be too low (as when your organization is able to finance more than one project), or, more commonly, their figures are higher than your supporters can, or will, give you in one year, or in a capital pledge-taking drive, in three years.

2. A goal, particularly for a capital drive, is not set by the head of an institution, or by the finance committee, or even by the board of directors without both an internal and an exernal survey, or feasibility study. See Chapter Eight.

Now for the positive rules.

1. Your organization must have a clearly defined need. This need, or needs, will be the basis for your "statement of the case." See Chapter Eleven.

2. These needs must be "salable." They must be items or programs that your constituency will recognize as justifiable and be willing to help you attain. It is difficult, often impossible, to build support for a pure ideal. The public must be able to see the practicality of the ideal before they will buy in.

Several years ago a major church denomination in America voted at its annual convention to raise one million dollars for a peace effort. The vote was nearly unanimous, for the cause had been presented in a stirring manner. Later a critic said to me: "That drive will never be successful." "Why?," I queried. "Because the sponsors have no plan as to how to spend the funds. Most everybody is for world peace. But few people will give until they know what their money is to be spent for."

The critic was right. Very few dollars were raised.

3. The body of potential donors must be clearly delineated. Thought must be given as to who is apt to respond. If you plan, for instance, a direct-mail appeal, and need to purchase a list of potential donors, you would not buy a random list of five thousand, or fifty thousand names. You would be selective in your purchase (see Chapter Thirteen). Nor would you approach a rod and game club to support a drive for gun control.

4. The financial ability of your list of prospects is of utmost importance, and must be carefully studied. This does not mean that only the affluent will support your cause. Sometimes the people of moderate means will be your best contributors. But it does mean that some persons are able to give more than the large majority and should be approached accordingly.

5. The dollar goal must be established within the range of financial ability of your prospect list.

6. *Interest*, as well as *ability*, must be a determinant in goal setting. Unless you can capture the interest of your readers or audience, their financial ability means little.

HOW TO RATE

One way to rate a membership list is by their past record of giving. This method follows the established principle that new money is found wherever gifts have been received in the past. It is a principle that cannot be neglected. Yet it is insufficient, and exclusive application of this guideline may jeopardize your drive. When the Covenant Presbyterian Church of Fort Myers wished to study their list of potential major givers prior to a capital campaign, they drew up a list of the top ten percent of their donors. From this list they wished to secure the workers who would call upon their more affluent members. After my arrival we conducted a rating session such as described in this chapter. We then drew up a second list of "top ten percenters," based this time not on their past record of giving but on their *ability* to give. The two lists were quite different, and a new list of potential callers in the campaign had to be drawn up.

Had the church used only the prior listing, they would have raised much less than the $455,000 actually pledged.

Prepare Flat Lists of Your Prospects

A flat list is, of course, a series of pages of prospects, twenty or more names per page. I prefer twenty-five names and addresses per 8½ x 11 sheet, though I sometimes use legal size (8½ x 14) with thirty-five names. On the right side of each sheet will be two columns (sometimes three) with headings to be checked or filled in by various persons.

Names are to be typed alphabetically, by families or giving units, rather than by individuals. Be sure to have correct addresses, with zip numbers.

Many organizations will at some point in their campaign wish to enroll volunteers to call every prospect by telephone. Such calling is usually done to build up attendance at a promotional dinner or event. If desired by your group, type phone numbers on these flat lists for later use.

Place all names of your prime list—members or alumni or active supporters—on list A. List all nonmembers or nondonors on list B. This B list is usually run off on colored paper to make easy

Form 15–1

RESOURCES LIST   Page No. 1

No.	Name and Address			Phone Number	Would He or She Make A Good Visitor?	Estimated Giving Potential
1	Mrs. Colin Adamson 32-B Village Dr.			393–3467		
2	Mr. George Ainsleigh 82 Church St., Apt. 3-A			393–8131		
3	Mr. & Mrs. Richard W. Allen, Jr. 56 Juniper Brook Rd.			393–3923		
4	Miss Jane Arbour 25 Colby St.			393–2073		

the differentiation from list A. You may wish to type onto a C list all nonresidents. Use of C list makes it easier for you to treat these persons in a different manner, for example, more mail or special types of mailings.

The kind of information you desire will determine the columns you place on the right hand side of your sheets. Do you plan to use many volunteers, such as making calls in the homes? If so, set up a column one-half inch wide entitled: "W–L" for indicating which names would make good workers and which good leaders. Use of this column is essential if you need to recruit many workers.

The most important column, of course, is the column used for financial ability, headed "Estimated giving ability."

I do not give out any information, such as amounts of previous gifts, since I do not wish to influence any judgments. I prefer beginning with a blank tablet. There are occasions, admittedly, when the disclosure of previous gifts might be useful, but such information should be restricted to a small group of not more than seven or eight persons.

A sample of the flat list is Form 15–1.

The number of flat lists to be prepared is dependent on their use. I prefer a committee of twenty-five persons to help me rate. Since I will have various other uses for these lists, I prepare fifty copies.

Invite a Committee to Rate

It is imperative that you invite the proper persons to rate your lists. Do not use only staff. In a school do not use only administrative staff or faculty. Such persons are too close to the institution and tend to judge other people by their own interest. Thus they rate too high. Also they are often too optimistic about the ability of persons that they know only through class reunions or committee work. You must be sure that your raters include a majority of persons representative of the persons you will be soliciting. Only they can accurately gauge the interest of your constituency.

Your raters must know many persons, especially through business relations. Thus older business leaders are ideal. Avoid those persons who are living on the edge of subsistence, for they have little conception of how "the other half" give to causes which interest them. Homemakers, too, tend to think in terms of the weekly family budget and thus their judgment is limited. Use some women, assuredly, but only those who are leaders—socially or otherwise—in the community.

It is wise to invite twice as many as you desire to attend. If your cause does not have many supporters, you will need even more leeway and will need to work harder to get out your required attendance. I usually aim for twenty-five or thirty raters.

It is important that the right person invites these prospective raters. This should be someone of influence, often the head of the institution or a prominent trustee. The invitation need not state the full purpose of the meeting. Usually my invitations state: "Come to help us set a proper goal. The meeting will last not more than ninety minutes."

At the rating session for the 1970 building campaign of the Kingswood School in West Hartford, Connecticut, twenty-five men were present. One of the leaders quietly whispered to me: "There is the vice-president of so-and-so insurance company. There is the owner of the largest men's clothing store in the area, etc., etc." The reason we had such an outstanding group present was the inviter—Henry Roberts, at that time President of the Connecticut General Insurance Company. All business leaders wanted to associate with Henry. When he invited, they came.

The results of this rating session were impressive. On our flat lists were 2,066 prospects, divided into 972 Old Boys (alumni), 324 parents, and 770 friends. From this rating list we identified almost 1,000 names that might be able to give $1,000 or more, in a three year pledge period. These high rated names, after eliminating the trustees, further divided into:

- 42 rated at $25,000 and up
- 97 rated at $10,000 to 24,000
- 207 rated at $5,000 to 9,000
- 606 rated at $1,000 to 4,900.

This rating was the foundation stone of the entire campaign. Out of it developed:

1. the campaign goal, later set at $1,500,000
2. the list of almost 1,000 special gift prospects
3. the division of the campaign into these five phases:
   a. Board development to receive pledges from trustees and a very few top prospects
   b. Leadership gifts—$10,000 up
   c. Challenge gifts—$5,000 to 9,900
   d. Special gifts—$1,000 to 4,900
   e. General gifts—below $1,000.

Each of these five divisions had its own chairman, its own workers, and its own schedule. Each division kicked off at different times, beginning with the highest rated group. There was some overlapping in the schedules, but all were timed to complete their calling within six months after announcement of the campaign.

Conduct the Meeting Efficiently

Thought must be given to the setup of the room for the meeting. There must be tables to work upon. Avoid long rows of tables and do not crowd them together. I like to scatter them about the room, with no more than four persons at an eight or ten foot table. This is to discourage conversation, or copying of one another's figures. We strive for objectivity and anonymity.

The head person of your organization should preside. He or she welcomes the attendees and makes a brief, concise statement on the purpose of the meeting—to prepare for the new program, to set a campaign goal, to make a list of campaign workers. This talk should be motivational. If it is a campaign for a new building, architect's plans may be shown, but only briefly. The architect should NOT be invited, since the purpose of the meeting is not to discuss plans, but to emphasize one subject only—rating.

If the campaign is organized at this point, have the chairperson speak for about two minutes.

The all-important instructions for the meeting are given by the development director, or by professional counsel. Instructions must cover four points—why rate, how to rate, averaging the ratings, and goal setting. Instructions must be given simply, clearly, and concisely. Allow two or three minutes for questions, but do not hold up the actual rating process by trying to satisfy all inquirers. One or two unbelievers at this point could prevent the rest of the attendees from performing their task. I sometimes state: "You may have further questions, or misgivings, but you will find that your questions become resolved as you get into the work. Let us now begin."

By far the preferred way to rate is by the meeting just described. Sometimes it is difficult, or impossible, to set up such a gathering. In this case you hand out your rating (resources) sheets, with a set of instructions (modified from the list following), and request return at a definite date—say in one week. WARNING. It is very difficult to get these lists returned to you. You may need to drive around to homes or offices to pick them up. If so, give your raters twenty-four hours notice, for you will discover that many of your raters have not yet begun their work.

Give Detailed Instructions

The instructions given to your raters must cover the following points. You may wish to duplicate and hand out to those present:

1. The purpose of rating is twofold:
   a. to set a campaign goal
   b. to determine who the larger givers will be
2. Attendees should not work as a team, but as individuals. Do not discuss any information. Work in privacy by scattering around the room.
3. The rating is to be confidential and objective. Do NOT sign your work sheets.
4. Check lists for accuracy. Change wrong spellings and addresses. Cross out the deceased. If you do not know the new address, at least cross off the old. Add names which are prominent by their omission.
5. The first assignment is to secure leadership. Check the names of those who would make either a good leader (L) or a good worker (W).
6. The second assignment is to give an estimate of what each person COULD give, if sufficiently interested.
7. The individual ratings should be for the campaign period, whether for one year or three years.
8. The question to be asked is all-important. It is not: "What *should* he or she give?" It is not: "What *will* he or she give?" It is rather: "What *could* he or she give if sufficiently interested." Emphasis must be upon ability—upon the COULD.
9. Avoid uniformity. Consider each name as unique. No appraisal is valid which rates every name the same.
10. Do not guess. Base each rating upon some knowledge, no matter how slight.
11. Omit rating names you do not know.
12. Do not be concerned about rating names too high or too low. Remember the other raters in the room. Some will be higher, some lower than you. We are seeking *averages* of all estimates made tonight. The goal will be based upon the total of all averages.
13. Begin by rating yourself. This is not a pledge, since you do not sign your work. Ask yourself: "How much *could* I give to this program?"
14. Next, rate someone in the room. Perhaps the chairperson or chief administrator. Could he or she give as much as you, or more, or less? Put down a figure.
15. Finally, go to the beginning of the list and put down a figure

for every name you know, asking always: "What *could* this person give if interested?"

16. You may leave when finished. Some will finish long before others. Place your lists on the head table, face down.

Average the Ratings

The figures from your raters must first be collated, so that you can prepare to determine averages. I use a form similar to Form 15–2.

You will save much time if you can persuade eight or ten of the raters to remain after the meeting to collate. They work in pairs: one reads from the individual rating sheets and the other records the figures on the form.

You need not retype names onto these Summary Sheets. Cut up one set of rating flat sheets and paste the column of names onto the one set of Summary Sheets. Or, place the number beside each name on the rating lists onto the Summary Sheets to identify each set of figures.

The averaging is most easily done with a calculating machine having a tape printout. Have a volunteer do each sheet as it is collated. Or, do it yourself in the morning.

Review the Averages

Experience with ratings points out that a few persons will be overrated, and thus their figures should be scaled down. I try not to have any person rated beyond his or her ability, since it is a morale booster to the donor who is able to say: "I gave the amount suggested."

Many more persons, however, will be underrated, and it is essential that their figures be raised. Underrating usually occurs when there are several persons serving as raters whose ability is a good deal less than many in the room. It is difficult for a person who can give only $25 to realize that others can give $1,000 or more. Thus their ratings pull down the averages.

Hence the need for a review committee.

The review committee is made up of your financially more able people, particularly those who know many others. The head of your institution should serve, and one or two of your most knowledgeable trustees. A banker or two is excellent. And perhaps a lawyer or stockbroker. There should be six or seven of these who will meet for three or four hours one evening (more, if your list is over a thousand names).

RESOURCES—SUMMARY SHEET

MAS-TER LIST NUM-BER	INDIVIDUAL ESTIMATES																																								TOTAL OF ESTI-MATES	NUM-BER OF ESTI-MATES	AVER-AGE ESTI-MATE	FINAL ESTI-MATE
	1	2	3	4	5	6	7	8	9	10	11	12	13	14	15	16	17	18	19	20	21	22	23	24	25	26	27	28	29	30	31	32	33	34	35	36	37	38	39	40			

Note: When reproducing this form, enlarge to width of 17"

It is most helpful if the developlment officer makes an opening statement, dealing in general terms with what he or she has noted and advising about procedure for this evening's work. The instructions I gave to the review committee of the Fort Myers Church were:

Review Committee Guidelines

1. A *few* names will be rated too high and must be *reduced*. Especially where only one or two or three ratings are given.
2. *Many* names will be rated too low, particularly those who have ample means.
3. The concept of COULD must be adhered to. It is the purpose of the campaign to raise their interests from moderate or lukewarm participation to enthusiastic sharing.
4. Keep in mind—in a very few cases, especially the elderly wealthy—of the possibility of a "once-in-a-lifetime" gift.
5. Sometimes—in a *few* cases—we give a range: "10,000 to 20,000." Do not overdo this.
6. Sometimes the *highest* figure recorded is put down by the rater if this person was present at the rating meeting.
7. It is sometimes helpful to begin with the pastor's name, or the chief executive, and then relate other names accordingly.
8. Names not rated by anyone at the rating meeting may be nominally reviewed at $1.00 per week.
9. For the very top names (eight to ten), you may wish to write in the name of the best person to call.
10. SPEED is essential, since there are over 500 names. Therefore,
    A. Beware of the human tendency to make nonfinancial statements about interesting names, stories of golf, tennis, etc.
    B. Do not discuss names rated at $5.00 or LESS. Leave the average where it is, unless it is very evident that the name is underrated.
    C. Spend very little time with ratings between $5.00 and $10.00. Reason: a change from $6.00 to $7.00 or $8.00 means very little.
    D. Spend most time with highest rated figures.
11. The one secret—discount.

The one secret I have in every campaign is the amount which the total of the averages is to be cut back in setting the goal. If the rating group has done its work well, the total of their averages will be too high to reach in your campaign. This is so because the concept used by the raters—could give—is somewhat idealistic.

Their prospects *could* give the average amounts, but many will not. And, also, allowance must be made for prospects who are never interviewed or who are not called upon a second time when more time is desired.

Experience demonstrates that a well-run effort will reach about 50 percent of the total of all averaged figures. Thus the goal is set at one-half the amount of the averaged appraisals. It is essential that this discount figure be kept undisclosed, for if it gets out, most persons will say: "I need give only one-half my suggested figure."

I sometimes wonder whether to tell this 50 percent figure to even the small review committee. Generally I find it necessary, since the usual review committee tends to say: "Charley *could* give $3,000, but he'll only give $1,000. So put down $1,000." My task is then to repeat that we are working on the concept of *could*, and that the 50 percent discount allows us to do some speculating. "If," I state, "he *could* give $3,000, it is up to us to motivate him. So let us challenge him with the $3,000 figure." It must be made clear, however, that we do not rate any person at twice the amount he or she may be able to give. We challenge him or her with a figure that may be high, but never too high, to be reached.

Set the Scale of Gifts Needed

It is standard operating procedure to draw up a scale of gifts needed to reach your goal. This is not generally needed in a church campaign where the giving ability of members is better known and hence reliance can be made upon the suggested figure only. But in more widespread drives the scale is essential, and the more you publicize it, the better,

Here is the standard scale used. Begin with this and then adjust to fit your constituency:

Number of gifts needed	Size of each gift	Total amount
1 gift	10% of total goal	10%
2 gifts	5% each	10%
4 gifts	2½% each	10%
8 gifts	1¼% each	10%
etc.	etc.	etc.

As you double the number of gifts on each level, you cut in half the percentage of total goal needed from each donor.

The cardinal rule is to begin by thinking of securing one gift at ten percent of your goal. This is not always possible, but you must initially give thought to it. If the goal be very large, and the resources of your constituency limited, you may need two or three gifts to reach your top ten percent of goal. You then proceed down, visualizing a pyramidal shape, and trying to fill in each level of the pyramid. Your scale might then look something like this:

Scale of Gifts Needed for $100,000 Goal

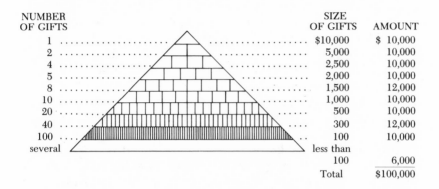

NUMBER OF GIFTS		SIZE OF GIFTS	AMOUNT
1		$10,000	$ 10,000
2		5,000	10,000
4		2,500	10,000
5		2,000	10,000
8		1,500	12,000
10		1,000	10,000
20		500	10,000
40		300	12,000
100		100	10,000
several		less than 100	6,000
		Total	$100,000

See Form 19–7 for a scale used in a campaign.

A scale of gifts is essential for a large goal. It can also be used for a modest drive. The First Baptist Church of Westwood, Massachusetts, set a goal of $1,000 for a world relief offering. Here is the goal drawn up by my wife, with actual results:

Size of gifts needed	Number needed	Number received	Amount received
$100	1	1	$ 100
75	2	1	75
50	3	2	100
35	—	1	35
25	4	6	150
20	5	2	40
15	—	1	15
10	9	12	120
5	12	17	85
3	—	3	9
2	15	26	52
misc.	—	several	221
			$1,002

One year later the Westwood Church stepped up its gifts to $1500, with top gifts of $300, $200, and two at $120.

Set the Value of the Share

The use of the share concept is an attempt to guide the giver—especially the small giver—in determining his or her gift. If the giver believes in your cause, he or she wants your campaign to succeed, and thus wants to give his or her proper share to do his or her part. But here the prospect needs help. He or she does not want to give too much, or too little. What is this person's fair share of the entire goal? The campaign which does not help this prospect is hurting its own cause as well as failing to help the prospect.

Most successful campaigns today make suggestions for donors to consider giving. This is commonly done by suggesting the gift of a share, which carries a specific dollar value. Many campaigns do not call it a share (churches sometimes ask for a tithe, the ancient Biblical practice of giving 10 percent of one's income), yet there often is an implied share or suggestion.

The value of a share may be different for every organization and every locality. It must make sense, and appeal to, the majority of donors within your group or society. It should be a little high, but not too high, for the majority to reach. A quick rule of thumb would be to skim off the top 10 percent of your total anticipated gifts and determine what would be the average needed from the bottom 90 percent of your givers to reach your goal. Then, since you never get all your prospects to give, you set the value of the share at perhaps 20 percent above the average gift needed from this 90 percent.

If your organization is somewhat more affluent than an average similar society, the value of your share should be set slightly above the average gift of the lower 60 percent, or 75 percent, of your expected gifts.

The danger of the use of shares is that, if wrongly used, the more prosperous of your clientele, well able to give more than a share, will peg their gift at the share. This is avoided by the use of multiple shares. Many persons are urged to give a share. A few persons are urged to give two or more shares. The multiple share principle is further explained in Chapter Nineteen.

Use of the Average Figure with Major Prospects

The third reason for rating is to arrive at a figure to suggest to the larger giver. This figure is used only by the major gift (or advanced pledge) committee, since the majority of prospects will be asked to contribute a share. The amount to be suggested serves as a threefold guide:

- pointing out the major prospects so that they can be given extra attention
- indicating which of your prospects require your very best solicitors. Your president cannot call on everyone. Whom then does he or she call upon? Those persons capable of the largest gifts usually respond at their highest level only when called upon by either a personal friend or by the head of the institution.
- showing the larger donors the need for a few leadership gifts if the goal is to be reached. The organization which leaves the size of the very highest gifts entirely up to the donor, without any guidance, is flirting with failure.

Step 8—Rating the Prospects—is the most difficult procedure to "sell" in fund raising, and the most productive when properly used. Omit this step with the greatest of reluctance. It will be costly to do so.

CHAPTER 16

Step Nine:

Cultivating the donor

That institution—or group—which keeps its constituency informed is generally the one which receives the greater financial support. The basis for cultivating the would-be donor is printed matter, both periodical and occasional. Special events are an essential element if the organization is in a position to invite the public to visit its buildings or grounds. Most valuable, though of necessity limited in scope, is the personal attention given to a small group of influential supporters.

Every organization seeking public support must have a carefully thought-out program of informing—and thus cultivating—its donors. This program is directed at both present and future donors. It begins with wide dissemination of the printed word, continues through special events, and culminates in personal attention given to a small group of your most influential constituency.

GUIDELINES FOR CULTIVATION

Cultivation is the process of gaining the prospect's attention, winning this person's active interest, and culminating in his or her partnership through sharing of time and resources. It is brought about through printed matter, special events, and most importantly through personal attention.

There are certain basic concepts that must be adhered to, regardless of the avenues of communication. First is an identification of the person's interests with those of the appealing institution. What are the gut feelings of the donor? What will give this person the greatest satisfaction in helping you? In a church campaign, for instance, it is remarkable how a simple, but fundamental, concept can lead to generous giving: "We are not giving to a budget. We are giving to God." Likewise for a social or artistic cause: "We are giving to children, or young people, or elderly."

The second concept grows out of the first. The objectives of your organization must be in line with the donor's concerns. Does your group have high aims? Do they make sense? Are they attainable, at least in part?

The third concept might be the personnel of your organization. Do your leaders reflect sincerity—a deep belief in what you are doing? Are they able to project both enthusiasm and a certain hardheadedness in pursuing goals? The active seeking of partnership in your work will find a response.

Your cause should be prepared to be of assistance to your friends and would-be supporters. This may be the fourth criterion.

Finally, you must work to earn the prospect's friendship. This will take time for those brief, chatty phone calls and personal notes and for an occasional luncheon.

PUBLICATIONS

If you desire continued and new backing, your organization is obligated to keep your supporters informed. The public has a vast capacity to forget, which is neutralized only by a flow of information. The beginning of the cultivation process is the printed word, which gives you the broadest possible avenue of communications. An even wider means may be the use of radio or television, but these media may not be available to the vast majority of nonprofit groups because of cost or not reaching the proper constituency.

This book's use of the term "printed word" includes any type of duplication—multilith, mimeograph, photocopying—as well as the printing press. There is a use for most of these processes, dependent upon your need for speed, informality, and economy. The ease by which clear copy can be duplicated today has largely replaced mimeographing in fund raising. Increasingly popular is the employment of "photo-ready" copy run off by those new shops especially set up to handle short runs of typed or hand-lettered copy in an hour, or while you wait. Your only requirement is to submit neatly prepared copy. Use of an electric typewriter is considered obligatory.

The means of using the printed word include both periodical and occasional publications.

PERIODICALS

If your institution has an established publication, by all means use it. Begin with an early conference with the editor, agreeing on such details as:

- kind of copy, whether news, announcements, or block ads
- how often you will submit copy, and deadlines
- length of copy
- use of photographs
- when your fund raising calls for special emphasis
- the cost, if any.

One of my favorite means of communication is the newsletter. I like it because it is fast, can be newsy (if properly timed and well written), is inexpensive, and is completely under my control. I believe it can have a broad readership, often wider than a letter. It can be prepared in a half day, but is better if allowed to age for a few days. Have at hand a file into which you place brief notes on events, persons, or announcements. Then open the file one or two days before your deadline to assemble and space properly. It is imperative that a newsletter *look* attractive, as well as be well written.

Too many newsletters are poorly prepared, are dull reading matter, and far too wordy. Use these guidelines for your newsletter:

1. Copy must be as written for a telegram or cablegram where you pay for each word. Eliminate adjectives and articles.

2. After first copy is written, go over it again, marking out all superfluous words and phrases.

3. Avoid the obvious. Eliminate all "preaching." Good copy, based upon sound accomplishments, tells its own story. Moralizing is not needed, and is objectionable.

4. Short copy is essential. Leave details for other types of publicity. Determine the length of your normal newsletter and stick to it. My favorite length is one sheet of 8½ x 11, typed on both sides. Sometimes I run two sheets (four sides); never more. In an emergency—or times of good news—I will send out a newsletter

of one page only. I prefer colored paper (the same color for each issue), especially chosen for printing both sides without "bleeding" through. Though not necessary, I often have my printer run off thousands of sheets ahead of time, containing our masthead (always with telephone number) and space for addressing, with postal permit number. Keep masthead and address space on same side of sheet to save printing costs. Use of this "self-mailer" eliminates need for an envelope. Use of envelopes is optional.

5. Set up a mailing schedule ahead of time. My favorite timing is a monthly. If you establish the same date each month for mailing, you will discover that your newsletter acts as a spur to complete many other tasks in order to write them up for publication deadline.

OCCASIONAL PUBLICATIONS

Each campaign, whether for annual funds or for capital, must have its distinctive piece. This piece, whether as simple as a folder to fit a Number 10 envelope, or a brochure of eight or more pages, often 8½ x 11 size, must be designed especially for its particular drive. The folder for the smaller drive may be very simple, sometimes a photocopy of a typed piece. It is more usual, however, to have it set in printer's type and offset. Color is generally effective. The cheapest way to obtain color is to use colored paper (always pastel; dark colored paper is too difficult for older eyes to read) with black or dark brown ink. A new press, able to do inexpensively five colors on two sides in one run, is the Biddie-Glazer press.

Photographs add interest, providing the quality of print is good and not too many persons are in the picture. A good rule to follow is not more than four to six persons.

Quality costs money. The brochure for our Fort Myers campaign had to be printed in less than a week. The printer said it could be done, but that we would be disappointed in the reproduction of our colored photograph for the cover. What would he suggest? I was, I stated, willing to run all errands. The printer said there was only one photographer and shop in the city equipped to take the quality of photograph we needed. Shortly before noon I called upon the proprietor and told her my predicament. "If the sun stays out this afternoon," she replied, "I'll have my cameraman take the picture and you can pick up the print at 4:00 P.M. tomorrow." The sun cooperated, the photographer and developer rushed their work, and the printer delivered us a four color brochure. It was expensive to do it this way, but the finished booklet was pleasing to everyone, and it helped the campaign raise a good deal more money than thought possible.

There are as many different ways to write a brochure as there are campaigns. Since, however, I usually write my own copy, often do my own layout, and am always engaged in six other projects at the same time, I have simplified the outline I follow. The order I adhere to in the majority of my campaigns follows. This will win no prize for originality, for layout, or for fine writing, but it is easy for the reader to follow, it tells the essential story, and it (acid test of all) raises the funds needed.

1. A brief history of the work or institution. Usually one-half to a maximum of one page.
2. A story of the problem, greatly simplified. Is it a need for greater operating funds? Then stress the *additional* funds needed, rather than the total needs.

Is it mortgage reduction that you seek? Then set forth the interest money you will save. Is it building remodeling or enlargement? State your present problem, such as costs to do patch-up work, costs of heat leakage, or water damage, inconvenience to classes, and programs you cannot undertake because of lack of facilities.

3. The solution proposed becomes the lead story—usually the center two pages.
4. Copy directed at the reader concerning his or her own giving— the need for all to raise their sights and the opportunity for each to give through a call in the home.
5. Statement of amount of the goal and scale of gifts needed. See Chapter Twelve.
6. A page (or half page) of questions and answers. One question must deal with suggested amounts to give, often called a share. See Chapter Fifteen.
7. A listing of names of all campaign leaders and workers.

Larger campaigns, or more involved drives, call for additional inserts placed immediately prior to the center spread statement of the proposed solution to the problem, or immediately following.

When seeking major gifts, it is essential that at least a half page be devoted, following the center spread, to a chart of the scale of gifts needed to ensure reaching the goal. See Chapter Twelve.

It is customary in capital campaigns to design a basic brochure (or case statement) that can be adapted for use either by major donors or by general givers. Production costs are greatly reduced by designing one page (near the end of the brochure) for the major giver. This page sets forth the scale of large gifts needed. For the smaller giver, this one page is replaced by another page which tells of the share plan of giving.

Here is the page-by-page outline our twelve-page brochure in Fort Myers followed:

1. Four-color photograph, exterior of church on front cover
2. Photograph of courtyard of church, people entering
3. "Our History"
4. "What Excites Us about Covenant Church?"
5. Messages (with portraits) of minister and chairperson
6–7. (center two pages) "Opportunities of Expression toward Thee." A statement of interest savings, plus what might be done with this savings. Two photographs of children at activity tables.
8. Scripture passages, plus picture of baptism of child
9. Three brief paragraphs on:
   Raising our sights
   Pledging in the homes
   The goal
10. Answers to questions, and the names of campaign workers
11. Photograph of courtyard—people leaving church
12. Back cover (in color)—two more pictures of church (interior and exterior)

All photographs were in black and white, except two covers. There was no use of color in rest of brochure.

Too many campaigns fail to order enough printed copies. There are apt to be many other uses of the brochure, such as giving to friends, to libraries and newspapers, and to members joining in the future. Order extra. The additional cost is negligible.

SPECIAL EVENTS

The staging of special events, in order to advertise your society and its work, is a most effective manner of cultivating present and future constituencies. Two results can emerge: (1) the presence of the public on your home grounds, or at some gathering sponsored by you, and (2) the publicity that the event engenders.

If your institution or group has an attractive building or grounds, the public's curiosity can be diverted to your advantage. It is helpful to get old friends and new acquaintances to come see something of your property, particularly when you set forth your aims and accomplishments at the same time. Would an open house be appropriate? If so, arrange one annually. If your program cannot be presented on your grounds, what about setting up some type of assemblage to tell your story? There are many places you can rent—perhaps your public school auditorium or cafeteria—to hold a display or at least a public gathering to listen. Have you thought of renting a tent? Tent rental agencies have space heaters so that these areas are comfortable in all but the coldest of winter.

Thought must be given as to what audience you wish to reach in any special event. Will you invite all prospects, or only those capable of giving $1,000 up, or only those few super prospects? The type of event will differ in each case.

In launching its campaign, Union College felt the need to gather her leading alumni to bring them up to date on current trends in the college and to tell them of the coming campaign (there would be no solicitation). Because of its location, the college decided to hold two events, one a leisurely two days on campus, and the other a one day affair in New York City where many alumni worked. The invitation list was restricted.

When the United Presbyterian Church in the U.S.A. held its Fifty Million Fund drive, the churches around Stronghold, Illinois, decided to hold a special gift dinner in a former home of a Chicago magnate. The house was built as a stone castle. It was agreed to use a medieval theme, and although the sponsoring nucleus was unsuccessful in finding a whole suckling pig (apple in mouth) for the center table, they did rent costumes of the Tudor period, including hennins (steeple headdresses) for the women waitresses, and lackey suits for the men who met the guests and parked their cars.

Benefit performances have been held at theaters for scores of years. They may fit your program and your locality, but they are dangerous. Often the net returns are so small as to question the benefit for the energy expended. A benefit sometimes leaves the public with the belief that they have adequately supported your work. Another question is whether it would not be more useful to put on your own evening's program once your friends have gathered. A benefit performance may well attract persons who might not attend a program of your own making, but the reverse is also true. In the long run this second group should prove to be more steadfast friends than those who come only for entertainment.

Events, of course, can be very simple, beginning with tea for two in a home or office. Luncheon or dinner meetings have long since proven their value. Sometimes they can be arranged when nothing else can. An associate of mine, responsible for a hospital

100

campaign in New York City, spent almost two years trying to figure out a way to get the drive going by telling the hospital's need in a more personal way than the printed word. At length, after trial and error, it was discovered that a series of luncheons for the very top prospects was an effective way to obtain large gifts—a luncheon in a private dining room of the hospital attended oftentimes by only the hospital administrator, a surgeon or research doctor who told of his or her specialty, and the prospect. It was a long, drawn out affair, but it worked in obtaining very large gifts when nothing else did.

A dinner, either complimentary or subsidized, followed by a presentation of needs, is a very popular procedure. If you desire a crowd, you will need to work to build attendance. One written invitation, or public announcement, will not do it. You should either set up a telephone brigade to urge attendance, or plan a series of novel mailings. When one college set up an alumni dinner in New York City, I arranged a series of mailings: first an explanatory letter six weeks ahead stating date, purpose, and a complimentary dinner. Then once a week for five weeks we mailed postal reminders. These cards were specially printed, with postal permits, giving a different, brief message on each card. To ensure reading, each card had a humorous illustration which tied into the theme. Results: over 900 attended, the largest gathering off-campus for the college in its history.

Publicity is the second important reason for holding special events. Think of publicity in several modes:

- radio and television news
- newspaper stories
- your institution's publications
  periodicals
  newsletters

Since the reading audience of events reported by the public media is far greater than any group you will be able to get together, it could be that the reporting is of greater significance than the event itself. Keep in mind, however, that the wider public informed by public media are not as a rule donors. There will be donors among them, assuredly, but they must be sought out for their gifts. Think of publicity not as a fund raiser in itself, but as a preselling aid, as a preliminary to solicitation. Publicity generated by a financial drive can benefit your cause in many ways, some of which may be long range. Seek it out. Help generate publicity. But do not count on it doing your fund raising for you.

PERSONAL ATTENTION

It is a perennial problem of the fund raiser to determine how much time to devote to giving personal attention to the more affluent constituency. A related problem is how to go about it—what type of attention to plan.

The fund raiser, regardless of title, must be easily accessible to the public. This person must be sensitive to the possibility of his or her job intimidating the body of his or her supporters, and will continually strive to be open and approachable. Unlike other administrators, his or her door must remain open. An associate once remarked to me: "That man will never be a good development man. He keeps his door closed." The undue interruptions of a few busybodies can be controlled by an alert secretary.

Human it is to forget. Dates and times. Events. Institutions and good causes. Even during an intensive six week drive, I continue to be surprised by the number of persons who forget. The reason is simple: people are preoccupied by their daily jobs and their families. All other causes must work to achieve remembrance.

We cannot force a person to open a letter. But we can make sure the letter—or letters—which give the essential information have been sent. And we can, with a limited number of leaders, follow up with phone calls.

Letter writers should avoid the stiff, formal presentation that does not reflect the spirit of your enterprise. Seek out what is unique, or newsworthy, and insert these elements into each letter. If your mailing is large, add a postscript to at least some of your letters. If very large, work with your printer or mailer to put on a uniform P.S. Some readers will look only at the signature AND the P.S.

Avoid the continual appeal for funds. Some of your letters or publications should omit any mention of need. Treat your reader as though he or she were a friend, a friend who is worthy of sharing your joys. When this spirit is cultivated, the appeal, when it comes, will be given more heed.

Now and then we hear some person of affluence state: "Everyone is after me for my money. I want to be liked for myself." This feeling seems to be especially true of the retiree who is not challenged by daily work, or by the homemaker. It is a feeling we need to appreciate. Every now and then we should send out a personal, handwritten note for no ostensible reason. Dr. Dale Turner, affable minister of the University Congregational Church of Seattle, sat with me at a doughnut shop counter one day. The next day he said that he had written a personal note to the counter man. "Did you know him previously?" I asked. "No." "Then why did you do it?"

"When I was a student in seminary," he replied, "I resolved to send a handwritten note every day to three persons expressing some appreciation. Every day since, for over thirty years, I have kept up this practice. I get some amazing responses."

A personal telephone call occasionally, when there is no reason for the call, might be of great benefit to your cause. Such phoning could, of course, be overdone and interfere with one's daily production requirements.

We all like to be asked for our opinions or advice. There is a danger, assuredly, of seeking advice in such a way that the giver is disturbed if the advice is not followed. Yet we tend to err too much in not seeking counsel. One of the finest ways to compliment a person is to seek his or her advice. We should utilize this human trait by asking persons to serve on committees or to assist in making various studies. Following such an appointment with liberal use of names in publicity and reports is a simple way—often overlooked—of building loyalty.

One of finest ways to cultivate a person is to appoint him or her to serve on your board.

One veteran fund raiser has gone so far as to say that large gifts are usually obtained *after* the donor has been appointed to the board of trustees.

Placing the names of larger donors in public places—on a building, on a room, on a wall plaque—is one way to thank a supporter. Most of us like this recognition. We have done more than aided a good cause. We have attained a type of immortality—keeping our name alive after our death. Yet this procedure is more than thanks to the benefactor. It is also a method of cultivating the prospective giver, for it implies that some day this person can have his or her name so displayed. I sometimes say to our larger givers: "I would like to publish your name. Not primarily to thank you. And we *are* most grateful. But primarily to influence other would-be donors."

CHAPTER 17

Step Ten:
Building an organization

The role of the volunteer is crucial in any drive for funds. The volunteer not only reduces staff payroll but also multiplies staff efforts, spreads the word of work being done, gives creditability, is a source of enthusiasm and tends to become a most loyal financial backer. Following the lead of the board, the volunteer gives primary direction to the funding drive. One becomes the general chairperson, who recruits a core of competent leaders to form the general committee. Each member assumes a particular responsibility and together they give general guidance to the entire campaign.

Funding for nonprofit organizations is greatly dependent upon volunteers. They can make or break almost any campaign. Careful thought must be given to their selection, to their assignments, and, finally, to their training and supervision. Review Chapter Five for general principles in using volunteers.

TYPES OF VOLUNTEER SOLICITATION

There are endless lists of work that volunteers can perform, but in the field of direct solicitation these tasks fall into four categories:

Letter Writing. Although the personal letter, often from one friend to another, is little used, there are rare occasions when this approach is essential. Far superior is it to 100 percent use of form letters.

Answering Telephones during a Radio or Television Appeal. These persons, most essential to this enterprise, are, however, merely order-takers. It would be impossible for them to persuade the person calling to give any figure higher than the amount he or she has in mind.

Phoning during a Telethon. Here the volunteer initiates the call. The workers usually gather in one room equipped with a bank of telephones. Each is given a list of names, with phone numbers, to call, requesting a gift or pledge. This system is best used by a school or college calling alumni toward the end of the year. It is, indeed, the clean up of a campaign, used only when the member, or alumnus, has not responded to previous appeals.

Soliciting Person-to-Person. This "eyeball-to-eyeball" approach is the most difficult to arrange on a large scale, but is productive of the highest results. If your organization is limited to one city or neighborhood, and can be organized for personal solicitation, you will benefit from this system. This is particularly true of a drive for capital gifts. But even if your organization is widespread, you should attempt to make a few calls personally. This minimum should include your trustees and your very top donors.

One of your earliest decisions in any campaign is the type of solicitation you will make. The rest of this chapter deals primarily with person-to-person solicitation and how to build the organization needed.

NAMING THE GENERAL CHAIRPERSON

Once you have decided upon having a campaign, and agreed on the goal, the most important choice left for you is the securing of a chairperson. A wrong choice for this spot can cripple your effort. The right choice not only greatly relieves the development director of many time-consuming decisions and much foot-dragging on the part of volunteers, but eventually makes a difference in the amount raised.

What are his or her qualifications? The general chairperson will be one who is recognized by all as a real leader in the community—one whose word carries great weight with others. He or she will need to be generous of time and money. Combined with experience in organization of people, this person must have a genuine concern—better yet, passion—for the cause he or she will represent. The chairperson's giving ability need not be of the highest, provided he or she can enlist a major gift chairperson who will be of top financial ability. Aim high in the business or professional world when you seek out this person. Go for the busy, successful executive.

The campaign chairperson is often found in your board of trustees. This was the procedure followed by the Massachusetts Council of Churches when seeking a chairperson for its drive a number of years ago. It was decided to ask Richard Higgins, chairman of the board of the Kendall Company. The asking committee was three: the executive director Forrest Knapp, Mr. Higgin's bishop, and I. After the challenge had been put, he answered: "Niel, if you had asked me, I would have said: 'No.' Forrest, if you had asked me, I would have said: 'No.' But I cannot say 'No' to my bishop." Dick Higgins became one of the greatest supporters the council ever had.

It is generally wise in looking for a general chairperson to make a list of half a dozen possibilities. Then, in consultation with others, list them in order of preference. Go to number one and tell this person he or she is your first choice. If he or she refuses, your selection committee can then go quickly to number two, and so on. Never, never recruit by letter or telephone. The securing of the right person is so crucial that it deserves all the time a personal call takes.

The first assignment of the general chairperson is to name a general committee.

THE GENERAL COMMITTEE

Overseeing the entire fund-raising effort will be the general committee, authorized by the board of directors. This committee will be responsible for the entire campaign, supervising such details as:

- engaging professional counsel, if such be required
- setting up a budget and authorizing expenditure
- determining the goal
- drawing up the time schedule
- approving major pieces of publicity
- enlisting volunteer manpower.

The entire committee should not be named by the board or chief executive. They do name the chairperson, and then, in consultation with him or her, approve his or her choice of the rest of the committee.

The chairperson will name, as the heart of the committee:

1. The special gift (or advance gift) chairperson, who recruits workers to call on the larger givers—often 10 percent of the prospective donors.
2. The organization chairperson who recruits workers to cover the remainder of calls—usually 90 percent.

These three persons comprise the strength of your campaign. Choose them with extreme caution. A larger campaign will require additional chairpersons, such as to direct the solicitation of trustees, and to direct corporation giving. Other members of the general committee are given in Chapter Six.

I prefer that each member be given a specific assignment. If you follow this suggestion, the need for meetings of the general committee will be greatly reduced, since each subchairperson names whatever associates or helpers he or she needs.

Think in terms of three objectives as you plan how many workers to recruit for soliciting special givers and general givers:

– enough so that no one is burdened
– enough so that the giving of the workers will be a significant amount
– enough so that as many persons as possible get involved. It is often said that the perfect campaign would be that which put every prospect to work.

It is unwise to ask one person (especially the chairperson of general gifts, sometimes called the organization chairperson) to enlist a large number of persons, particularly if their assignment be to make solicitations. Many years experience proves that an ideal objective is the "rule of four"—asking a leader to recruit four others. Try to avoid anything more than the recruitment of five persons, unless it be for such a task as making telephone calls.

TWO CATEGORIES
OF WORKERS

Except for that organization which raises funds by requesting the same amount from each prospect, every organization should have two types of workers as a minimum:

- special gift (or advance gift) workers who, themselves in the larger gift category, solicit those persons able to give in the larger amounts. If you have never used this breakdown of solicitations before, think in terms of 10 percent of your top prospects for this category.
- general gift (or smaller gift) workers. These solicitors, regardless of the size of their own gift, will call upon those able to give smaller amounts. Think of 90 percent of your entire donors in this category.
- in a limited number of cases, where the prospects are capable of a wide range of donations, you might have a small third category of very top givers, sometimes called major givers.

Each group of workers (major, special, general) has its own chairperson, its own set of workers, its own schedule, and its own objectives. See Chapters Six, Eighteen, and Nineteen.

Charts for the enlistment of solicitors is given in Chapters Six and Eighteen.

CHAPTER 18

Step Eleven:
Recruiting workers

Reaching a high goal is dependent upon personal solicitation, which calls for many volunteers. But people seldom volunteer to raise money. How then do you go about securing a sufficient number of solicitors?

Volunteerism lies at the center of good fund-raising. No organization can afford the expense of having paid help do all the work. Nor should it miss the luxury of the enthusiasm—and increased gifts—which the volunteers bring to the cause.

The use of volunteers usually requires greater time to recruit. But this is simply a problem of timing, and your schedule must allow for this.

Volunteers sometimes require more careful checking of their work. But usually this is solved by having a few very dependable volunteers assigned ahead of time to review the work of other volunteers.

Volunteers can be used to do various internal jobs dealing with checking of lists, mailings, etc. Most important is the use of volunteers in soliciting gifts.

VOLUNTEERS FOR OFFICE WORK

The summoning of volunteers for office work cannot properly be left to the director. The director must assign this task to a volunteer coordinator who first composes a list of willing workers, and then assigns them days and hours of work, as the director, day by day, requests aid.

The Covenant Presbyterian Church of Fort Myers was most fortunate in having a large number of retirees in the community who had the time to give. And in having Clarissa Harrison as the coordinator. Before the seven week campaign ended, Clarissa had supervised the appearance of fifteen women (and a few men) who donated several hundred hours of work. Their work, ranging from running errands to the post office, to checking changes of addresses, to making display posters, saved the church several hundred dollars. Even more valuable, they enabled the doing of many small details which, because of time pressure, would have otherwise been left undone. This extra attention to details added up to many increased pledges to the campaign.

Clarissa's procedure was simple, yet effective. She first secured the names and phone numbers of persons willing to work in the office. She then checked with the campaign director or secretary on a daily basis:

- Will you need help tomorrow?
- In morning or afternoon?
- How about two days—three days—from now?
- What type of work will it be:
  - typing?
  - stuffing envelopes?
  - correcting addresses?
  - recording figures?

It is amazing how work loads vary—even within a day. Often you cannot use volunteers in the morning because preparation of forms and letters are not complete. But by 3:00 P.M. you are in trouble if you do not have help in getting out a large mailing.

Experience has shown that in a fast moving campaign (is there any other kind?) the secretary or chairperson does not have time to make a half-dozen phone calls to secure emergency help. One phone call to a well-organized coordinator does the trick.

VOLUNTEERS FOR SOLICITATION

Of all ways to raise money, the most effective—the most productive in *size* of gifts—is the personal, eyeball-to-eyeball approach. This is the method used in the call in the home—or across the desk from a business executive. Such an appeal is far and away superior to all other methods.

The second most effective—again in terms of the *size* of the gift—is the appeal made to a group of persons around a dinner table, or in a meeting hall or church. This method contains certain pitfalls which must be faced ahead of time:

- The person making the appeal may not be at his or her best that night, due to a cold, or weariness, or long-windedness, or lack of enthusiasm.
- The attendance of prospects can be drastically reduced because of weather, conflict of dates with another event, or insufficient promotion to build up attendance.
- The enthusiasm of your crowd can be adversely affected by a dull opening program or by such details as a poor meal or inadequate service.
- It is difficult to put before your people suggestions about size of gifts desired—larger donations from the more affluent, smaller donations from others.
- It is impossible to answer questions of more than a general nature.

The third most effective solicitation is the telephone call. This has the advantage of being personal and being able to answer individual questions or objections. It has the disadvantages of no "eyeball" presentation and of not being able to carry away the pledge card or the check.

When I entered upon semiretirement I found it necessary to cut down on my contribution list. One casualty was to be one of the educational institutions I had attended. For two years they received no gift. Then the phone rang one evening. A call from a student at the university three hundred miles away. Would I give to the Annual Fund? I was impressed. I resumed my giving.

The least effective solicitation in size of gift is the direct-mail appeal. Its advantages are the far greater number of donors that are approached, the cheaper cost per response, and, usually, the speed of the appeal.

PREPARING FOR A
PERSONAL CALL

The requirements for personal solicitations made in the home or office are:

1. EFFECTIVE SOLICITORS—good salespersons for your cause. The size of individual gifts differs according to the effectiveness of the caller. He or she must not be a mere "order-taker," one who merely collects an amount—often of small size—that the prospect had already decided upon. The solicitor should be able to influence the donor to give more than the easily-arrived-at figure. Many a campaign has failed to reach its potential because the caller was the wrong person in certain cases. A study of results at the conclusion of any drive, especially a capital fund drive, shows that certain workers bring in uniformly low gifts and others turn in consistently high gifts. The careful selection of callers, particularly in the advance or major gift phase, is paramount.

2. MATCHING OF PROSPECTIVE DONORS WITH SOLICITORS who have already pledged or given within the range desired from the prospect. Peer calls upon peer. It is difficult, if not impossible, for a thousand dollar contributor to secure a ten thousand dollar gift. Water, states the seasoned fund raiser, cannot run uphill. In a large capital fund campaign this matching can consume many hours. It is, however, one of the very best uses of the director's time.

Calling for a large gift is not child's work. It calls for much preparation, much thinking ahead, a great deal of tailoring one's presentation to the interests of the would-be donor. The caller must "psych" himself or herself up. At times I have had callers tell me after holding a card several days: "I am not the person to make this call. Please reassign it." I always honor this request. In one campaign I reassigned one card to five different persons before the call was made.

3. SUFFICIENT NUMBER OF CALLERS so that no one worker is overburdened. The ideal is to have one worker for every five calls. You cannot always get this many workers. If not, you do one of two things:

– Increase the number of calls per worker to six assignments, but never more. There are often a *few* workers willing to make more than five or six calls, but do not give them any extra cards until the first five or six are completed. Avoid asking *every* worker to take several extra cards. They may do so this time, but you may have lost them for any future calling.
– divide your list of prospects into two: those to be called on and the remainder to be solicited by mail.

I was asked to step in to save a campaign that had floundered when the trustees of a girls' independent school had decided to conduct their campaign without professional help. After a year the board saw that volunteers without professional direction was not working. My first day on the field I called on a very active trustee, dedicated, one of the best fund raisers in the city. "I'm glad to see you," he greeted me. "I have here my cards and I shall call upon them." He rummaged in his papers, and it took him a couple of minutes to find a stack of pledge cards. "How many do you have?" I asked.

"I believe there are fifteen here."

"How long have you had them?"

"Eight or nine months."

"How many calls have you made?"

"None. But I shall."

I would like you to give them all back to me. We'll start all over again."

"No, sir. I took these cards, and I shall be responsible for them."

I had touched his pride.

"Art," I said, "I am not singling you out. I am asking everyone to surrender their incompleted cards, and then we'll begin again, and each worker will take only five or so cards."

"Well, if everyone gives back his cards, then I shall. Here they are."

In the reorganization Art, and every other worker, selected five cards and within a short time the goal was reached.

BUILDING YOUR WORKERS' ORGANIZATION

You must first determine how many workers you need to cover all cards—allowing each caller about five cards. Dividing by five is easy.

But if you need more than seven or eight callers, you must build an organization based on army principles:

- for every four callers you need one captain or key person
- for every four key persons you need one division leader
- you begin at the top and work down. Your organization chairperson first recruits the division leaders. YOU NEED ONE DIVISION LEADER FOR EVERY 100 CALLS TO BE MADE

– each division leader then recruits four key persons
– each key person then recruits four workers.

Thus each division leader directs the enlistment and performance of twenty persons, covering one hundred calls.

Do NOT request any person to recruit more than four or five
other persons. The task is too difficult. Use the table just given.

Sometimes the organization chairperson states that he or she
will save the strongest people for the bottom tier—the workers who
will do most of the calling—since they are the best salespersons.
This is a mistake. For the recruitment of workers is such a crucial
task that it must be entrusted to your most aggressive leaders. If
you do not choose your best persons as division leaders and key
persons, you will not succeed in getting enough workers.

Division leaders need help in securing the best available key
persons. Do not leave each division leader to enlist his or her key
persons without guidance. Experience proves that friendship, or
chance selection, is not good enough in enrolling top leaders. Key
persons, especially, need help in recruiting their teams, for at this
level every organization runs thin in number of persons able and
willing to work.

The simplest way to assist division leaders and key persons is
to begin with your prospect list—or your membership roll, if you
have one. The most committed workers come from those closest
to the inner workings of your group. Seek the assistance of a group
of friends of your cause. Have them check lists of your prospects

a. the few top leaders who would make good key persons
b. the larger number of persons who would make good callers,
but perhaps are not good supervisors

Chapter Fifteen gives further guidance in preparing lists of
prospective workers.

I then place each name and phone number of a prospective
key person on a 3 x 5 *blue* card. At a gathering of the division
leaders I distribute these blue cards, asking each division leader
to select about eight cards, from which he or she is to recruit four
key persons.

I then place each remaining name of a prospective worker
(including the blue cards not recruited as key persons) onto a 3 x
5 *white* card. I set a deadline of a week or ten days to secure the
key persons. Then I gather them together and distribute the white
cards among them, each key person selecting about eight cards,
from which he or she is to enlist four team members.

The organization chairperson must closely observe this selection process, for at some point one or more key persons will be in trouble in securing a full team. Organization chairpersons can request the division leaders to help one another with surplus names. He or she will also keep a master list of all prospective workers, and an organization chart of all leaders and workers as they are recruited.

The organization chart used by a church which was preparing to make a call in every home is shown in Form 18–1. Any organization can use this form. Note that the division leader recruits four key persons, who in turn recruit four workers each. This division of twenty-one persons is designed to cover 100 calls in the home or office. Make another form for each additional 100 calls.

Form 18–2 is a simpler form used by the advance pledge (or special gift) chairperson to recruit a committee of ten or twelve persons.

The organization charts should be prominently displayed. They will prove of inestimable help:

   – to show to everyone your progress in filling the workers' organization
   – to point out quickly where your weak spots are
   – to assist you when it is time to assign calls to workers.

COVENANT PRESBYTERIAN CHURCH

FORT MYERS, FLORIDA

1979

Team Roster for Organization Chairman: Bob White

DIVISION LEADER _____

1. Key Person _____

      1. _____

      2. _____

      3. _____

      4. _____

2. Key Person _____

      1. _____

      2. _____

      3. _____

      4. _____

3. Key Person _____

      1. _____

      2. _____

      3. _____

      4. _____

4. Key Person _____

      1. _____

      2. _____

      3. _____

      4. _____

Note: Use one sheet of this form for every 100 calls to be made.

COVENANT PRESBYTERIAN CHURCH

FORT MYERS, FLORIDA

ADVANCE PLEDGE WORKERS FORM

TO BE FILLED OUT BY ADVANCE PLEDGE CHAIRMAN: GARY HUDSON

Telephone:　Business – 334–5253　Home – 936–3298

The following have agreed to serve in our church enlistment as advance pledge workers. They will be present at the Advance Pledge Dinner at 6:30 P.M. on Monday, November 5, place to be announced.

WORKERS	BUSINESS PHONE	HOME PHONE
1.		
2.		
3.		
4.		
5.		
6.		
7.		
8.		
9.		
10.		
11.		
12.		

Note: Retain one copy for your records.
Return one copy to the Campaign Office.

Campaign Director
Niel Pendleton

CHAPTER **19**

Step Twelve:
Training workers

Training of the volunteer worker is mandatory for explaining the purpose of the drive, such as whether the gift to be sought is to be cash or pledge, the timing for solicitation, and reporting procedure. Most drives have three levels of workers, requiring different levels of instruction: the new worker needing a full presentation, the experienced worker needing reminders, and all workers being exposed to new procedures. Preparation and use of various forms will expedite the step.

WHY TRAIN?

Every drive for funds, using volunteer workers, must hold training or "refresher" meetings. This is true even for annual appeals, since the need for funds, and the goal, change from year to year. And, even the best of us need reminders. The training session is especially required by the capital drive since its thrust—and its financial goal— is greatly different from the annual appeal.

The experienced worker sometimes resents "training" sessions. Because of this we often call this session an instruction or refresher meeting. It is important that some type of get-together be held preliminary to making all calls. Such a meeting not only allows all workers to get acquainted with one another, and with the officers of your organization, but it also sets forth:

1. *The purpose of the drive.* The would-be donor wants specifics—is the drive for repairing the roof, for paying off the mortgage, for increasing salaries, for scholarships? The solicitor unacquainted with these details can be embarrassing to the cause and to himself.

2. *The type of gift desired.* Is it cash? pledge? for how long a period? Are there suggestions for giving? What are they?

3. *Timing of the drive.* When is it to close?

4. *Reporting procedure.* Where are results to be turned in? In what manner? What type of reporting, other than financial, is desired?

There are three types of workers who require assistance. First is the new or inexperienced volunteer who is willing to help, but needs detailed instructions and training. The organization which requests volunteers, and then does not adequately train them, is harming both itself and the volunteer. For each volunteer wants to do a commendable job. Morale is heightened as he or she realizes that training has helped him or her contribute to the success of the entire campaign.

Do not assume that the assistance you give to a young worker is too elementary. The holding of any question-and-answer session for workers quickly reveals the low level of understanding and expertise of several workers in the room.

The second type of worker is the veteran of many fund-raising appeals who sometimes needs special prompting to attend the training meeting. This worker *does* need reminding of goals, dates, and reporting procedures. And his presence, I suggest to him, is desirable to lift the spirits of the younger workers present.

The third type is *every* worker who is being exposed to new procedures. Perhaps it is the first time your organization is going for capital funds. In most such cases there are many unanswered questions. The explanation of the "why" of the campaign calls for full discussion when the workers get together. Do not slight this eagerness of your workers to obtain fuller information. Only as they become informed can they become enthusiastic salespeople. Especially imperative is the training meeting when the "suggested figure" for each donor is used for the first time.

HOW TRAIN?

Preparation for the Training Meeting

The preparation for this session involves five steps. These steps cannot be done the night before. Some of them may require weeks to accomplish.

First: the prospect list must be divided into at least two groups—the advance or special gift group, and the general or smaller gift group. This twofold division is a minimum, since the size of your prospect list, and the widespread financial ability of these prospects, may call for a third grouping, or rarely, even a fourth grouping.

Second: the division of your prospect list is obtained via the rating process. This step is a difficult one if your constituency is not well known, particularly if they are widely scattered. It is also a step that sometimes meets opposition when first presented to a closely-knit group such as a club, church, or temple. Yet it is a step that is crucial to any effort engaged in raising large sums. See Chapters Fifteen and Sixteen for details on rating your list and how to handle the resultant divisions.

Third: the pledge card must be carefully prepared to include these items:

a. name of campaign and name and address of organization
b. description (in six or seven words) of purpose of campaign
c. table of suggested amounts to give—often called shares
d. date of first payment is sometimes stated
e. space for designating gift, if desired
f. space for date of pledge
g. space for signature
h. a detachable stub which carries either name or master list number of prospect, with space for signature by person who agrees to make the call

Decision must be made as to how many types of pledge cards are to be used, such as:

– major givers (color A)
– special or intermediate givers (color B)
– general givers (color C)

– nonmembers or nonalumni (color D)
– nonresidents, or mail prospects (color E)

It is wise procedure to have pledge cards printed well ahead. In a large drive there will be much handling of pledge cards before the worker ever sees them.

Sample cards are shown below (Forms 19–4, 19–5, 19–6, 19–9).

Fourth: certain aids must be prepared ahead of time for the volunteer. The first aid is some type of visual which sets forth the pertinent points involved. These visual aids fall into several classifications:

– Blackboard, perhaps the simplest type. Can be very helpful for a small group, but has a disadvantage of lack of organization if not carefully planned.
– Sheets of paper mimeographed or photocopied. Control of these sheets is often overlooked and thus the speaker sometimes loses his audience as they shuffle through several sheets. I usually arrange to have these distributed one sheet at a time.
– Posters or signs prepared ahead of time. Most effective if done by a professional sign-painter or art instructor. I have used them in sizes up to four by six feet, hung from portable blackboards, and requiring two persons to turn the sheets.
– Films. Can be motion pictures (cost makes this medium unavailable to most), overhead projections, 35 mm film strips, or 2 x 2 slides. You should use professional help in preparing these.

In setting up an alumni banquet at the Waldorf-Astoria in New York City, I arranged for the development office of Union College in Schenectady to process my 2 x 2 slides from copy I supplied. These slides were to accompany the president's address and thus had a major role to play. The development office assured me they knew what I needed. When the slides arrived the day before the event, I became uneasy, I knew not why. Taking them to a large photo processor nearby, I explained how I intended to use them. "These slides," said the professional, "will melt the instant that large projector at the Waldorf is turned on." "What is needed?," I asked, in consternation. "A special type of slide, mounted in glass, to resist the heat." "Can you provide them for me?" "Not today, or tomorrow," he replied. "Will you put someone on a night shift to produce them for me? They are essential to our program tomorrow night, and I would be most grateful if you did." He did. We paid for overtime. And the program (900 persons present) was successful.

Copy for these visual aids must be carefully prepared. If your budget and your timing allow it, you can have a professional firm provide a film strip with accompanying cassette tape that sets forth your entire training program. This process involves several weeks, and a sizable budget. I use it only when I have a large staff scattered about the country putting on simultaneous training sessions. Use of this type of visual aid does ensure a complete and uniform presentation by a staff of mixed ability. Most fund-raising organizations, however, will require a simpler visual aid.

The visual aid that can be prepared and used by an organization of any size is the overhead projected film or the 2 x 2 slide. The copy for the film can be set in type by a printer, who provides variety by setting type and printing onto colored paper, which is then filmed. Or you can make up handwritten copy by using special grease pencils. Or use an electric typewriter. In any case, first get instructions from a professional in this field.

In 1970 the Kingswood School of West Hartford campaigned for $1.5 million for a new building. The training slides were made by a printer setting copy on twenty varied color sheets, which were then photographed onto 2 x 2 film. See Form 19–3.

This visual aid is, of course, for a one-time showing. It is used at the workers' training session, accompanied by oral presentation, and followed by a question period.

The careful development director will not rely solely on this type of training. The human mind is too forgetful. Hence the director prepares a second aid, a printed or multilithed piece to be given out to each worker. Most helpful are these printed handbooks if they are designed to fit into a man's coat pocket, with the cover folded back inside to hold several pledge cards. For the copy we used in the Kingswood School capital campaign, see Chapter Twenty (Form 20–2).

Another visual aid is the question-and-answer sheet, considered quite essential in any drive. This may range from quality printing in two colors down to mimeographed sheets stapled together.

Form 19–1 is the question-and-answer sheet printed for the YWCA of Hartford, Connecticut.

A "carry" piece, carried by the caller to show each prospect, is often supplied. Most helpful are these pieces if designed to raise sights of the donor. Such was the card, size 4 x 5½, used by workers in the small gift category of the Hartford YW campaign (Form 19–2).

A most simple aid to the conduct of a smooth meeting is the agenda given to each attendant. I find that the distributed agenda aids in several ways: it shows that I am prepared and hence builds up confidence in me; it keeps me on the track, without forgetting any item; and it assists the volunteer in seeing the whole picture. A sample agenda is shown later in this chapter (Form 19–8).

WHAT IS MY SHARE?

If this is your question, the table below may be helpful. Experience of hundreds of capital campaigns shows that success is dependent upon many hundreds of persons giving a share (or more) in one of the following categories:

	12 Quarterly payments	3 Annual payments	Total
Achievement Share	$100	$400	$1,200
Development Share	50	200	600
Builder's Share	25	100	300
Basic Share	13	50	150

WHICH SHARE WOULD YOU LIKE TO GIVE?

Fifth: Preparation for the training session also requires a plan to build up attendance. The finest program is useless if few of the required workers are present, which all too often happens. So plan ahead for 100 percent attendance.

Attendance begins with the volunteer leaders, those who recruited the roster of workers. They must first of all attend themselves. This should be made clear from the very beginning of recruitment. Next, they must continually stress the date—and the importance—of the training meeting to all their team. Then each leader needs to remind his or her team by telephone within forty-eight hours preceding the event. It is best if this leader be required to report the expected attendance to the leader above him or her.

The development officer cannot leave attendance solely to the volunteers. This person must send out announcements of time and place when he or she writes welcoming letters to the workers as their names reach his or her office. Additional listings of the training meetings should appear in all your publications. And, finally, a reminder post card.

There is one final aid to a good training meeting—a complimentary luncheon or dinner (I have even had breakfast meetings when people find it difficult to get together). These meals serve other purposes also. They assist in getting your training meeting started on time. And, importantly, they are valuable in breaking down our normal human reserve, thus building a receptive frame of mind by the time the meeting begins.

Training the Special Gift Workers

Experience proves that it is exceedingly difficult to conduct one training session for both the special gift workers and the general gift workers. Why? (1) Because the special gift worker tends to be older, more successful in business or profession, and more experienced in salesmanship. I talk differently to these two classes of workers, playing down the techniques of selling with the special gift workers. (2) Because I stress with the special gift workers the need to seek large gifts. We spend much time talking about suggesting gifts, the size of which would frighten most general gift workers. (3) Because with the general gift workers I talk about securing shares. I do not want the special gift worker to think about shares, since the unit is too small.

Here is the agenda I commonly use in my special gift (or advance pledge) training meetings:

SPECIAL GIFT (ADVANCE PLEDGE) COMMITTEE MEETING

Presiding: Special Gift Chairperson

6:30	Dinner	
7:15	Introduction of Workers	
7:20	We Have a Big Task	Chief Executive
7:40	How We Can Reach Our Goal	Special Gift Chairperson
	By calling in every home	
	By suggesting an amount	
	By being good salespersons	
7:50	Who Are Advance Pledgers?	
7:55	When Do We Call?	
8:00	How to Make the Call	
8:40	Discussion	
8:55	Importance of Report Meetings—Why, When, and Where	
9:00	Distribution of Pledge Cards for Calling	
	To be selected by each caller.	

A Visual Aid for Both the Special Gift and the General Gift Caller

The development director responsible for the instruction of workers is wise if he or she does not assume that one printed piece—the statement of the case, or the brochure—is all the information needed on the WHY of the campaign. There is always the chance of the worker not reading this piece. So the organizer of the workers' meeting should prepare a second aid dealing with the WHY. This can be effectively done by use of visuals, combining both the "why" and the "how" of the campaign. See Form 19–3.

Getting Workers to Give Before Their Calling

One persistent problem in fund raising is how to prevent the workers from making any calls before they themselves have given. When this happens, the volunteers solicit with less conviction, with less enthusiasm. Too often they have not decided on the amount of their gift and so prove unreliable guides to others. There are two methods used to circumvent this happening. The first is to have a pledging period during the training meeting, following the presentation of the cause and the instruction, before anyone begins to leave. This is best handled by giving to each key person the pledge cards for his or her team and having that person, at a specified time in the program, ask his or her team members to pledge, or give, right then and there, returning the signed cards to the key person.

There is a better way, which, as usual, calls for greater planning ahead. This procedure is to call upon each worker in his or her home or office BEFORE the meeting. The calling on the worker is done by his or her key person, who thus makes four calls. By setting up appointments this can be done as quickly as four in one evening. Before this, the division leader must have called on the key person, and so on back through the entire leadership. At some point, of course, one person has to lead off. This is usually done by the chief executive, who then calls upon the general chairperson.

The last method may be somewhat cumbersome. It calls for the careful setting up of dates for early pledging, with all leaders thoroughly understanding the procedure. It has the disadvantage of early pledgers not being exposed to the inspiration and training of the instruction meeting. I have, however, seen it work beautifully. It is almost foolproof in getting each worker committed to a dollar figure before he or she begins calling.

The Special Gift Pledge Card

As each campaign should have at least two sets of workers—special gift and general gift—so too should each have different pledge cards. The reason is simple—and costly if not followed.

The general gift pledge card will suggest giving a share (see Form 19–9). Since the share is below the ability of the special gift prospects, your drive will secure a much smaller total if these prospects see the share card.

Therefore, there must be a special card for the larger donors.

This card can be very simple without any suggestion whatsoever. I prefer a card for the major givers that does make suggestions. These suggestions can be either *multiple* shares or stated dollar amounts in the larger categories.

It is customary to print the different cards in various colors, to simplify the handling and assignment of each category. If the campaign is for a club, church, or school, cards for nonmembers or nonalumni, may be printed in a different color, an instant key both to the caller and to the office.

The campaign of Kingswood School used Form 19-4 as their major gift card. There are no suggested amounts on the card, though each worker had a suggested amount to give verbally to each prospect.

For the capital campaign of the Covenant Presbyterian Church of Fort Myers we divided the calling into three categories: (1) the advance pledge, rated at $7,800 up (2) the intermediates, rated at $1,000 to $7,000, and (3) the general givers, rated at one share ($5 per week, $780 per three years) or less. These figures were all over-and-above giving to current maintenance.

The advance card, showing suggestions from ten shares ($7,800) to thirty shares ($23,400), is reproduced as Form 19-5.

The intermediate card, with suggestions from two shares ($1,560) to ten shares ($7,800), is shown as Form 19-6.

This campaign combined an appeal for two purposes—mortgage elimination and annual operating—and kept each fund separate, as shown on the pledge card.

For the Kingswood School special gift committee we supplied an additional piece, designed to aid in securing larger contributions. This card—Form 19-7—gave the scale of gifts needed (which scale was also included in the brochure), information which had come from the rating committee. See Chapter Fifteen.

Selection of Cards by the Special Gift Committee

It is of paramount importance that callers for the major prospects be chosen with great care. Many a worthy cause has received a nominal gift, or none at all, because the wrong person called on a top prospect. The guiding principle is that like calls upon like, that a major prospect desires to be called on by an equal in finances and prestige. It is extremely difficult for one who gives $10 to obtain $100 from someone else. Any time spent in matching givers with callers is valuable. The only exception to this rule is when the head of the institution makes the call. This person is often—because of his or her position—the most effective fund raiser available.

Form 19–7

KINGSWOOD SCHOOL

Scale of Gifts for Goal of $1,500,000

Number of Gifts	In the range of	Totaling
2	$100,000	$ 200,000
4	50,000	200,000
6	25,000	150,000
12	15,000	180,000
25	10,000	250,000
40	5,000	200,000
50	3,000	150,000
139		$1,330,000
Many Gifts Under	3,000	170,000
	TOTAL	$1,500,000

Keep in mind that calling for larger gifts requires knowledge of prospect, skill in presentation, and psychological build-up of the caller. In several different campaigns a large prospect card has been returned to me a few days later with the comment: "I don't feel right about this call." I never question a worker who feels he or she is the wrong person to make the approach.

Training the General Gift Worker

Long before the instruction meeting for the general gift worker begins, a decision must be made about how the pledge cards will be distributed (Note that pledge cards *always* have names and addresses typed, or plated on). There are three ways to handle the distribution.

1. Free choice of cards. Here the worker selects each call he or she is to make. For the small drive (less than 100 calls), you can arrange cards alphabetically on tables, allowing space for workers to gather without crowding. The larger drive requires more space for cards and workers. The best method is to use wall racks,

holding up to 100 cards each, similar to those used by YMCAs. These wall racks are prepared two or three days ahead, usually alphabetically. If divided geographically, each section must be clearly marked with the name of a geographical division.

Care must be taken in announcing the availability of cards for selection. All workers must be notified at the same time, otherwise a few insiders will select the better cards, sometimes leaving only poor cards for other workers. The opening of card racks to workers can either be done a day or two ahead of the training session or immediately following the session.

It is imperative that workers be instructed to fill in—and deposit with you—the stub of each card selected. Else you will not know who is holding each card. Such lack of information results in many calls never being completed. Volunteer workers require much checking at this point.

2. Assignment of all cards. This system allows the development director to keep all calls within a geographical area, or within one class of prospects, thus saving time of the caller. It is an efficient way of distributing all cards. Its disadvantage is that the caller may not know his or her prospects and hence be less effective.

3. Combination of assignment and free choice. This is my favorite system, since it assures my getting all cards distributed while allowing the caller some choice. The method I have found most effective is to make up a packet for each key person (or captain). If the key person has a team of four workers, I prepare sixteen to twenty prospect cards for him, or her, which gives four or five cards per worker. These packets are then distributed AFTER the training meeting, when the key person gives his or her team a choice of the twenty cards. Here, again, the key person must make certain that all stubs are signed and turned in.

Thought given ahead of time to seating arrangment will pay off. A small group calls for no special arrangement. A group of twenty-five or more should have assigned seats. I request all teams to sit together so that they get to know one another and thus build up team spirit. This allows the key person to check on attendance of his or her team (and, in turn, for his or her division leader to check). It also permits easy distribution of cards for the workers' selection.

The Agenda

The presence of several volunteers in a room makes necessary the careful preparation of an agenda. Too many such gatherings are poorly planned, with resultant criticism and lowering of confidence.

Set up your agenda in consultation with your leaders, agreeing as to who handles what. Place on the agenda the amount of minutes to be devoted to each item. This helps keep each participant from overtalking. Then multilith the agenda and give a copy to each attendant.

The distribution of agendas helps to set a tone for the meeting. It reveals that thoughtful preparation has been made. It helps the audience to understand the steps involved in the entire program. Form 19–8 shows a simple agenda. Footnotes can be added to stress any points desired.

The General Gift Pledge Card

A sample is shown as Form 19–9. Note the suggested shares.

Reporting Results to Date

The instruction meeting should be used as a place to report the amount raised to date. This procedure serves three purposes: it acts as a deadline for the advance worker to report, it informs the leaders of progress (or lack thereof), and it builds enthusiasm of workers as they see what has already been raised.

A scoreboard is essential. This can take two shapes: a form prepared for each worker on which he or she tabulates amounts as reported orally; or, one board up front, large enough for all to see. As reports are given orally by advance workers, someone records with chalk while another totals the individual items. The one-board system has the advantage of a permanent display for all who come by.

It is easy enough to tabulate reports for one meeting. When there are amounts from preceding reports, the process is more involved. Hence any report board must have these items:

Team name or number	# of cards reported	Previous report $$	Today's report $$	Total report $$
Jones				
Smith				
Brown				
White				
Total				

Additions must be recorded both across and down. Between meetings, the "Total" of the last meeting becomes the "Previous" of the next meeting, all other dollar figures being erased. It helps to call attention, at the close of recording, to teams reporting most calls made and highest dollars.

The amount of enthusiasm generated by this reporting system can be electrifying. When the Fort Myers Church heard that their work had resulted in oversubscribing by $50,000 their goal of $400,000, they burst into the doxology, sang it three times, and then marched out of doors to the church, singing "The Battle Hymn of the Republic." One new church member stated it was the most exciting meeting he had ever attended.

Importance of Report Meetings

Report meetings are imperative in any drive using volunteers, particularly when you are holding to a time schedule. Be warned that many workers will resist them, suggesting that "we save time by mailing in our cards." Do not agree. For report meetings serve several purposes:

- acting as spurs to workers to complete their calls
- informing both management and volunteers of progress
- revealing weaknesses in time to make corrections
- providing morale boosters to those workers who receive early turndowns.

Sometimes the special gift workers hold their own report meetings. Their results, however, need to be announced at meetings of the general gift workers.

The development director needs to keep close tabs on the progress of the very top prospects. When results come in early, he or she announces them only at the time and place where his or her institution will receive greatest benefit. If it is an intensive capital campaign, announcement is usually made at a report meeting of workers. This announcement often acts to raise the spirits of callers who still have solicitations to make.

In a short drive of four to eight weeks the first report from the advance workers can be made at the training meeting of the general gift workers. The next report meeting, usually one week later, is designed for both advance and general workers. Strive to avoid having a "drop-in" meeting—or even a tea or cocktail hour. Such meetings are too casual, especially in large cities, and do not exert enough pressure upon the volunteer to make his or her calls. Insist on setting up report meetings with:

– a definite day and hour
– in the same place each week
– a "sit-down" occasion, usually a luncheon, though it may be a dinner, or even a breakfast.

Use the scoreboard at each session. Encourage discussion of problems and successes. Provide opportunity for reassignment of cards. Urge workers to pick up another card or two to finish the task of getting all cards out. Be lavish in praise and thanks. And that afternoon or evening, mail out a typed report to *all* workers, both absentees and attendees. Indicate your leading teams and their dollar returns.

The reporting of twenty-five or more workers will be greatly speeded up by the use of report envelopes. The principle is that many workers can be preparing their reports at the same time. They place inside the envelope all cards being turned in, both pledges (gifts) and refusals. On the face of the envelope they fill in the prepared form, indicating number of cards enclosed, amount of each individual gift, and total dollars for the entire campaign period. The key person then deposits in the larger envelope the report envelopes of his or her four workers, filling in the face of the envelope with total number of cards and dollars from his or her team. Each division leader then deposits in the largest of all envelopes the report envelopes from his or her four key persons, totaling on the face the number of cards and dollars. All this, regardless of number of workers in the room, can be completed in about twenty minutes. When time to report, the chairperson calls upon division leaders only to report for the scoreboard. In drives of fewer than one hundred workers, reporting may be done by each key person. In using this system, no worker has to keep track of his or her previous reports. The scoreboard provides this information.

Forms 19–10 and 19–11 show sample report envelopes for workers and for key persons.

Mailing of Reports

It is standard operating procedure to mail out, following every report meeting, a mimeographed or printed report to each worker and to administration and perhaps trustees. This report goes to those workers present as well as to absentees. It serves several purposes. It shows progress to all, especially to absentees. It reminds absentees that others are at work. It compliments the teams reporting highest

YWCA
QUESTIONS AND ANSWERS
FOR THE BUILDING CAMPAIGN

1. WHY DOES THE HARTFORD YWCA NEED A NEW BUILD-
ING?

Because the YW has lost its residence and administration building
at Ann and Church Streets to the Trumbull Street Redevelopment
Project.

2. WHAT PROGRAM IS NOW BEING CARRIED ON?

The YWCA is operating out of several units in Hartford. Programs
are continuing to grow in our West Branch and East Branches. Woolverton Hall, on Broad Street, is being used for some classes and
activities, in addition to housing. The administrative staff is temporar-
ily housed at 119 Ann Street. Then we are using facilities of 13
institutions about the city for teen-club, handcraft classes, swimming,
etc.

3. HOW MUCH HAS THE YW PROGRAM BEEN CUT BACK
BY THE LOSS OF 262 ANN STREET?

A. Housing has been reduced from 207 beds to 126 beds.
B. We have no facilities for dances and our summer day camp
had to be reduced from 340 girls in 1969 to 117 girls in 1970.
We have no gymnasium or swimming pool of our own.
C. On the other hand, we have secured the use of pools and activity
rooms of many agencies, schools, and churches in the inner
city.
D. Although we cannot continue indefinitely without a central building, there are some advantages to our decentralized program,
for our staff is using this time to go out more into the neighbor-
hoods.

4. WHAT WILL THE NEW BUILDING PROVIDE?

Housing for 200 girls; an all-purpose assembly hall and gymnasium;
many multi-purpose activity rooms; lounges and offices, a swimming

pool; all in a ten story building with a two story program wing. There will be parking for at least 95 cars.

5. WHAT WILL HAPPEN TO WOOLVERTON HALL?

The cost of rehabilitation and incorporation into the larger building—plus the difficulties and expenses of supervising two residence halls—make the demolition of Woolverton the only logical step.

6. HAS ANY MERGER OF FACILITIES WITH THE YMCA BEEN CONSIDERED?

Yes, in 1967 a joint committee presented the following recommendation:

Increasing community needs for the services of both YMCA and YWCA and the need for replacement of, and additional, facilities led to joint exploration of all possible ways of economizing in the projected building programs of the two organizations.

The joint committee formed for this purpose included current and past presidents and long range planning chairmen of both organizations, so that detailed familiarity with their operations was available throughout the in-depth search for opportunities to reduce costs.

The committee concluded that staff economies are not possible in the obviously different kinds of programs provided by each agency. Similarly, any immediate economies which might be effected by a joint building program would soon disappear and would be restrictive of further expansion and of the flexibility required by the constantly changing social structure.

This joint study group is unanimous in this conclusion that the well-being of the various communities served by the YMCA and the YWCA will be best enhanced by separate facilities.

Representing the YWCA were Mrs. Robert Baxley, Mrs. Marshall Hoke, Mrs. Keith Hook, Mrs. Richard Park, Mrs. Douglas C. Scott, and Miss Ruth Thompson.

Representing the YMCA were Austin Barney, Philip Breux, Alan Cook, Richard Haskell, and Wilson Jainsen.

7. WHAT WILL THE NEW YWCA BUILDING COST?

Revised plans, greatly simplified from the original plans, will provide a building for $5,600,000.

8. HOW MUCH DID THE YWCA NET FROM THE SALE OF ANN STREET?

After purchasing the property at Broad Street and Farmington Avenue (adjacent to Woolverton Hall, our other residence building), and clearing the land, the YW has $500,000 remaining.

9. WHAT OTHER ASSETS ARE AVAILABLE?

The YW has in its investment portfolio $500,000 in undesignated funds that can be put into a new building.

In addition, the rental income from rooms in the new structure can amortize a long-term mortage of perhaps $1 million. Thus a total of $2 million is in sight.

10. WHEN WILL THE CAMPAIGN RUN?

Beginning November, 1970, and into the spring of 1971. We suggest a three (3) year payment of pledges, though some may desire four or five years to pay out. Capital giving is essential to success in this drive.

11. WHO ARE THE LEADERS OF THE YW BUILDING CAMPAIGN?

James A. Stewart, Senior Vice President of the Travelers Companies, is Chairman. Mrs. Richard B. Park is Vice-Chairman, and honorary chairmen are Charles P. Cooley, Jr. and Miss Amy O. Welcher. Mrs. Calvert G. Keirstead is President and Ruth A. Thomson is Executive Director. Other members of the Steering Committee are:

Mr. William G. Bates	Mr. Moses J. Neiditz
Mrs. Robert V. Baxley	Mr. Richard Rockwell
Mr. George Chase	Mrs. Douglas C. Scott
Miss Cornelia Gross	Mrs. M. Philip Susag
Mrs. John S. Gutman	Mr. Jack D. Taylor
Mrs. Bruce P. Hayden	Mrs. Edward H. Truex
Mr. David C. Hewitt	Mrs. Alan S. Wilson
Mrs. Frederic S. Hoffer, Jr.	

KINGSWOOD NOW

Why a campaign for Kingswood School?

Because Kingswood is among the top boys' schools in America. Over the years our largest number of graduates have been admitted to:

Amherst, Brown, Colby, Cornell, Dartmouth, Harvard, Middlebury, Princeton, Trinity, Williams, and Yale.

Last year a record of twenty boys out of a class of fifty-four were cited by National Merit Scholarships.

Because Kingswood continues its tradition of excellence
 – "to test each boy's mind and body . . . that his moral fiber be strengthened and his potential . . . fulfilled"
 – pupil–teacher ratio is ten to one
 – Kingswood continues its reputation of a school that innovates

Maintaining excellence involves "growing pains"
 1. Enrollment is growing modestly:
    1960—285
    1969—368
    1973—425
 2. Operating costs have spiraled:

	1960	1969
Average book cost	$ 4.00	$ 8.79
Scholarship aid	15,000	44,000
Salaries	203,000	448,000
Total Budget	342,000	778,000

Kingswood must provide new space for fine arts.
 Recognizing that self-expression is deepened through music, drama, and painting, Kingswood has only makeshift quarters— and that very limited—for practice and teaching in these arts.

The cost for a Science-Arts Building
$2,250,000

The preservation of private education is dependent upon
 – providing quality education
 – raising funds to support it

The recommended goal of
Kingswood Now
is $1,500,000

To raise $1,500,000 we must receive gifts in the following ranges:

	In range of	Total
2	$100,000	$200,000
4	50,000	200,000
6	25,000	150,000
12	15,000	180,000
25	10,000	250,000
40	5,000	200,000
50	3,000	150,000
Many	under 3,000	170,000
	Grand total	$1,500,000

Thus we see that in a successful campaign:
A few subscribers will give
50 percent of amount raised
About 10 percent of the subscribers will give the next
30 to 40 percent.
The other 90 percent of the subscribers will give the
remaining 10 to 20 percent in small gifts.

Kingswood has 2,750 prospects
1,530 Old Boys
450 Present Parents
770 Friends and Past Parents
Of these we shall call upon
1,000 in Advance Gift phase
1,200 in General Gift phase

Your Preparation

A. Read:
1. Campaign folders 1, 2, 3, and 4
2. Brochure (being mailed)
3. "Technique of Solicitation"
4. Worker's Portfolio
B. Plan your talk to fit your prospect

CULTIVATION OF PROSPECTS

A. All advance gift prospects have been invited to opening dinner
B. All will receive brochure
C. All will expect your personal call

THE CALL

Make each call "eyeball-to-eyeball"
Never solicit by telephone
Never solicit by mail

Tell in your own words:
Why Kingswood Now is important
Why YOU are supporting it
Be prepared:
To answer prospect's questions
If you cannot, obtain answers and see prospect later

Emphasize what prospect's dollars will do
Make a specific suggestion:
a room
a facility
a dollar amount

DO NOT SHOW the pledge card!
DO NOT LEAVE the pledge card!
If prospect is not ready, make appointment to see him or her again.
If second or third call is necessary, MAKE IT.

BEFORE CALLING

Sign your own pledge card
A generous response from your
prospects is influenced by a
generous response from you.

amounts. It allows opportunity to correct errors. It reminds all of the next report meeting. It reveals, without scolding, which teams are falling down, or at least are slow in turning in cards. Form 19–12 shows the simplest type of report. It is best if mailed out the day of the report meeting.

Form 19–4

In consideration of the gifts of others, I (we) hereby subscribe to Kingswood School, West Hartford, Connecticut, for the Capital Program, over the next three years:

$ ....

payable: (   ) Annually;   (   ) Semi-Annually;   (   ) Quarterly; or as follows:

Date ....   Signature ....

Card No. ....
Reported by ....
Total Pledge $ ....
Cash Herewith $ ....

Please fill in this stub, detach and return in Stub Envelope.
DO NOT TAKE THIS STUB WITH YOU.

Card No. ....

This card taken by:

Your name ....

Form 19-5

_____

In recognition of my time, talent, and treasure as gifts from God, I am happy to subscribe to Covenant Presbyterian Church, Fort Myers, Florida:

For THREE Years	For ONE Year
Mortgage Elimination and Capital Needs beginning December, 1979	Annual Operating Expenses beginning January 1, 1980
☐ 30 Shares = $23,400 ☐ 15 Shares = $11,700 ☐ 25 Shares = $19,500 ☐ 10 Shares = $ 7,800 ☐ 20 Shares = $15,600 One Share equals $5 per week for 3 years ($780) Total OR $_____ per _____($_____)	$_____ per week $_____ per month $_____ per year

Taken By
_____

_____

Date _____ 1979   Signature _____

This pledge may be changed by notifying the church office in writing.

Form 19-6

_____

In recognition of my time, talent, and treasure as gifts from God, I am happy to subscribe to Covenant Presbyterian Church, Fort Myers, Florida:

For THREE Years	For ONE Year
Mortgage Elimination and Capital Needs beginning December, 1979	Annual Operating Expenses beginning January 1, 1980
10 Shares—$7,800 ☐ 4 Shares—$3,120 ☐ 8 Shares—$6,240 ☐ 2 Shares—$1,560 ☐ 6 Shares—$4,680 ☐ One Share equals $5 per week for 3 years ($780) Total OR $_____ per _____($_____)	$_____ per week $_____ per month $_____ per year

Taken By
_____

_____

Date _____ 1979   Signature _____

This pledge may be changed by notifying the church office in writing.

AGENDA

WORKERS' TRAINING CONFERENCE

FIRST BAPTIST CHURCH
Needham, Massachusetts

Thursday, March 10, 1977

Richard Gates, General Chairman, Presiding

6:30 Invocation . . . . .Franz E. Oerth
6:31 Dinner
During the dinner each key person should fill out a report envelope, enclosing signed pledge cards from any workers. If you do not have cards with you tonight, please do *not* report them.
Advance pledge chairperson should also fill in a report envelope.
7:15 The Meaning of What We Do . . . . .Franz E. Oerth
7:25 The Report of Progress . . . . .Richard Gates
Reports from key persons
Report from Advance Pledges
7:40 The Steps Ahead . . . . .Richard Gates
Dedication Day
Making the Calls
The Report Meetings
7:45 How to Make the Call . . . . .Niel Pendleton
8:15 Discussion
8:30 Let Us look at the Pledge Card . . . . .Niel Pendleton
8:35 Closing Prayer
8:40 Distribution of Pledge Cards
NOTE: Be sure *not* to take away any pledge cards tonight *without* signing and tearing off stub on left hand side and giving them to Lucy.
ABSENTEES—Key persons should not use as workers anyone who has missed this training session, unless key person will give a training session to absentees. (It is largely a waste of time and resources merely to give out cards to an absentee.) There will be a brief make up for absentees this Sunday morning during coffee hour.

Form 19–9

In consideration of the gifts of others, I (we) hereby subscribe to Kingswood School, West Hartford, Connecticut, for the Capital Program, over the next three years:

(Check one box or fill in line below)

☐ Builder's Share $300   ☐ Development Share $600
☐ Achievement Share $1,200
OR $ ....

payable: (   ) Annually;   (   ) Semi-Annually;   (   ) Quarterly;
or as follows:

Date ....   Signature ....

Card No. ....
Reported by ....
Total Pledge $ ....
Cash Herewith $ ....

Please fill in this stub, detach and return in Stub Envelope.
DO NOT TAKE THIS STUB WITH YOU.

Card No. ....

This card taken by: ....

Your name ....

Form 19–10

WORKER'S

REPORT ENVELOPE

NAME _____

Name of Key Person _____

Date _____

INSTRUCTIONS

1. Be sure that the card for each subscription is correctly filled out, signed and dated. Attach cash or check payments to the pledge cards.
2. List each card on this envelope—last name with 3 year total for Mortgage Elimination and 1 year total for Current Expenses. DO NOT ADD TOGETHER THESE TWO FIGURES.
3. Put the cards, cash and checks in this envelope. Hand to your key person at report meetings.
4. Also turn in all other cards on which you have exhausted all possibilities of receiving a gift. Mark the reason on the back of the card—"deceased," "moved," "unable to find."

NAME OF GIVER	3 YEAR MORTGAGE	1 YEAR CURRENT
TOTALS		

Number of cards enclosed _____

Note: This envelope is for a campaign for two separate funds. Most campaigns will be for one fund. If so, eliminate one column above.

Form 19–11

KEY PERSON'S REPORT

NAME _____

DIVISION LEADER _____

DATE _____

HOW TO REPORT

1. Collect each worker's report envelope for your team.

2. Write the total report of the workers of your team in the spaces below. Then give this envelope to your division leader.

Number of cards enclosed _____

Total amount of each fund:

MORTGAGE ELIMINATION
(3 Year Total) . . . .$ _____

CURRENT EXPENSE (1 Year Total) . . . .$ _____

Note: This envelope is for two funds. Eliminate either fund not desired.

Form 19–12

	TRINITY CHURCH	
Oct. 7, 1979 Report	Northborough, Massachusetts	

We happily report these results from Sunday's meeting:

Total cards turned in	314
Renovations	$151,476
Goal	$150,000

Congratulations to Don Dodson's team high for Sunday night—$3,034. High team for total to date—$11,917 is Bob Bailey's. High Division for Sunday was Merrill Bergstrom's at $6,932. Merrill's division was also high for Total at $36,752.

We reached our Victory Goal, even though we needed the previous organ gift of $20,700 to do so. Congratulations to all leaders and workers who made this victory possible. There are yet 36 cards outstanding. Please complete all calls and turn cards in to the church office, marked for Ethel Cole.

TEAMS	RENOVATIONS # cards	Previous	Today	TOTAL
Creaser	13	$ 3,936	$ 876	$ 4,812
Perry	22	3,252	1,152	4,404
DeCiccio	25	6,570	360	6,930
Covel	9	3,213	25	3,238
MILES Division	68	16,971	2,413	19,384
Bailey	25	11,221	696	11,917
Braman	23	7,387	930	8,317
Dodson	22	4,227	3,034	7,261
Connor	32	6,985	2,272	9,257
BERGSTROM Division	102	29,820	6,932	36,752
Miller	20	4,137	—	4,137
Pratt	23	3,708	1,540	5,248
Seavey	27	6,878	1,700	8,578
Sanders	22	3,720	468	4,188
SANDERS Division	92	18,443	3,708	22,151
GENERAL GIFTS	262	$ 65,234	$13,053	$ 78,287
ADVANCE PLEDGES	52	$ 47,249	$ 4,840	$ 52,089
TOTALS	314	$112,483	$17,893	$130,376
Bank interest				300
Miscellaneous				100
Organ Bequest				20,700
				$151,476

CHAPTER 20

Step Thirteen:

Securing the gift

Maximum dollar is raised by one person talking to another, face to face. The caller must be well prepared—knowing much about the project and something about the prospect. During the interview the caller has to be persuasive and direct. This person should suggest the amount desired, directly or indirectly. The caller must listen, without necessarily being turned off, and must be willing to make repeat calls where helpful.

It has been said that campaigns fail (when they do), not because people did not give, but because they were not asked. Asking is the name of the game. Asking is far and away the mightiest tool in any campaign. It bears repeating that people do not give to causes, they give to people. They give to the asker. They give for other people.

The careful selection of the asker and his or her preparation, is of paramount importance. The recruitment of the proper caller, and matching with the would-be donor, are discussed in the preceding chapter. Here we deal with the solicitation itself.

Asking is an art. Some persons are superb at it, in part because of native ability. But everyone can develop this art through study and experience.

The first element required in learning the art is absorption in the cause you represent—a full understanding of the aims and accomplishments of the cause. Knowledge leads to belief in, and then to devotion to, and finally enthusiasm for, the cause.

The second element is the finesse that comes from experience. Reading of the successes of others will help, and, fortunately, there are many books and articles dealing with personal experiences in asking and the art thereof. Reading will also reveal what approaches, what words, to avoid. But the greatest aid is experience—learning by trial and error. Fortunate is that beginner who can accompany an experienced solicitor in making a call. Here I pay tribute to Louis W. Robey, teacher par excellence, whose many stories of his personal experiences, together with his patient setting forth of philosophy and techniques, was the foundation of my fund-raising career.

George Widener, of Philadelphia, and his son Harry went down on the *Titanic*. Harry, graduate of Harvard, had been an ardent bibliophile, and his mother visited President A. Lawrence Lowell to offer the university a gift of her son's 3,000 rare books. Harvard at the time was in need of a new library building. Lowell persuaded Mrs. Widener to give, as a memorial to her son, the present Harry Elkins Widener Library. In his will Harry's grandfather, Peter A. B. Widener, stipulated that his art collection should go to either Philadelphia, New York, or Washington. The National Gallery in the nation's capital won the collection, described as "one of the greatest events in the history of American museums." Perhaps that consummate fund raiser Lawrence Lowell influenced this gift, as well as the Harvard library building.

Psychologists state many different reasons why people give. It can become a complicated study indeed. But, it seems to me, we need remember but two of these reasons—the desire to benefit the general welfare by our gifts, and the yearning on the part of many for some type of immortality, brought about to some extent by the preservation of our names in connection with a gift—the Bodleian Library of Oxford, the Guggenheim Fellowships, the Cecil Rhodes scholarships, and thousands of others.

It is easy enough to be cynical about giving. Perhaps this is one way to justify refusing. It is a frame of mind to be avoided. There are, of course, gifts offered in hopes of some personal quid pro quo. Such offers can be—and usually ought to be—declined. But the overwhelming majority of gifts to philanthropy are based, not upon any tax reduction or personal benefit, but upon the desire to help other people. The seeker of funds will ever be guided by this humanitarian impulse found in so much of society. And especially in American society.

PREPARATION FOR
THE CALL

Preparing oneself for solicitation involves three levels. First is acquaintance with the general cause you represent and particularly with the objectives of the immediate drive. This knowledge is built up by attending instruction meetings and by conversations with leaders of the organization seeking funds. It is strengthened by personal involvement, as far as possible, with recipients of benefits afforded by the organization—the handicapped children, the needy scholars, the cured patients. It is to be hoped that acquaintance with the cause will lead to conviction of its necessity.

Not everyone has the opportunity for such personal involvement, but all can study the publicity provided. Particularly significant are the brochures and other pieces especially made for the campaign, a folder on questions-and-answers, newspaper or periodical clippings, and various types of film.

The second level in preparation is forethought concerning each prospect to be visited. The fund-raising institution may have a file on each major donor, or would-be donor. Conversation with friends or business associates of the prospect can give much guidance. When seeking such help, the solicitor should not request that his or her inquiry be kept secret from the prospect. It is often beneficial when the friend alerts the prospect, for this in itself is a step in the cultivation process. It is a cardinal rule in fund raising that the seeker never spring surprises upon the donor. As far as humanly possible, all steps in the asking process should be direct and above board.

I asked Mrs. John Washburn of West Hartford the secret of her success in obtaining several $10,000 gifts from nonmembers of her church. Her reply: "I treat everyone differently. I think of each one's interest and speak of that. If one is concerned with education or youth, I speak of our need for Sunday school space. If another is interested in music, I tell of our need for an organ or choir rehearsal room."

The third level is the concern over using proper techniques. Some methods seldom or never work. Others work most of the time. Finding out which is which is based not merely upon experience. There are written pieces which are helpful. Perhaps the best short piece, reproduced countless times in American fund raising, is the speech given by John D. Rockefeller, Jr., in 1933 before the Citizen's Family Welfare Committee of New York City. It merits full presentation here, as Form 20–1.

I have been asked to say a few words on the technique of soliciting donations.

Perhaps the best way to acquire a knowledge of that subject is to ask ourselves the question, "How would I like to be approached for a gift?" The answer, if carefully thought out, may be relied upon as a pretty safe guide to the task of soliciting. I have been brought up to believe, and the conviction only grows on me, that giving ought to be entered into in just the same careful way as investing—that giving *is* investing, and that it should be tested by the same intelligent standards. Whether we expect dividends in dollars or in human betterment, we need to be sure that the gift or the investment is a wise one and therefore we should know all about it. By the same token, if we are going to other people to interest them in giving to a particular enterprise we must be able to give them adequate information in regard to it, such information as we would want were we considering a gift.

First of all, then, a solicitor must be well informed in regard to the salient facts about the enterprise for which he is soliciting. Just what is its significance, its importance? How sound is the organization back of it, how well organized? How great is the need? An accurate knowledge of these and similar facts is necessary in order that the solicitor may be able to speak with conviction.

It is a great help to know something about the person whom you are approaching. You cannot deal successfully with all people the same way. Therefore, it is desirable to find out something about the person you are going to—what his interests are, whether you have any friends in common, whether he gave last year, if so, how much he gave, what he might be able to give this year, etc. Information such as that puts you more closely in touch with him and makes the approach easier.

Again, one always likes to know what other people are giving. That may be an irrelevant question, but it is a human question. If I am asked for a contribution, naturally and properly I am influenced in deciding how much I should give by what others are doing.

Another suggestion I like to have made me by a solicitor is how much it is hoped I will give. Of course, such a suggestion can be made in a way that might be most annoying. I do not like to have anyone tell me what it is my duty to give. There is just one man who is going to decide that question—who has the responsibility of deciding it—and that is myself. But I do like a man to say to me, "We are trying to raise $4,000,000, and are hoping you may be desirous of giving blank dollars. If you see your way clear to do so, it will be an enormous help and encouragement. You may have it in mind to give more; if so, we shall be glad. On the other hand, you may feel you cannot give as much, in view of other responsibilities. If that is the case, we shall understand. Whatever you give after thinking the matter over carefully in the light of the need, your other obligations, and your desire to do your full share as a citizen, will be gratefully received and deeply appreciated." When you talk like that to a man, he is glad to meet you again, and will not take the other elevator when he sees you in the corridor because you backed him to the wall and forced him to give.

Of supreme importance is it to make a pleasant, friendly contact with the prospective giver. Some people have a less keen sense of their duty and responsibility than others. With them, a little urging may be helpful. But with most people a convincing presentation of the facts and the need is far more effective. When a solicitor comes to you and lays on your heart the responsibility that rests so heavily on his; when his earnestness gives convincing evidence of how seriously interested he is; when he makes it clear that he knows you are no less anxious to do your duty in the manner than he is, that you are just as conscientious, that he feels sure all you need is to realize the importance of the enterprise and the urgency of the need in order to lead you to do your full share in meeting it—he has made you his friend and has brought you to think of giving as a privilege.

Never think you need to apologize for asking someone to give to a worthy object, any more than as though you were giving him an opportunity to participate in a high-grade investment. The duty of giving is as much his as is the duty of asking yours. Whether or not he should give to that particular enterprise, and if so, how much, it is for him alone to decide.

To recapitulate, then, briefly: know your subject; be so sold on it yourself that you can convincingly present its claims in the fewest possible words. A letter may well precede an interview, but personal contact is the most effective. Know as much as you can about the man to whom you go; give him a general idea as to the contributions being made by others in his group, and suggest in a gracious and tactful way what you would be glad to have him give, leaving it entirely to him to decide what he shall give.

> Be kindly and considerate. Thus will you get closest to a man's heart and his pocketbook.
>
> *These remarks were made by Mr. Rockefeller at a meeting of campaign workers for a project in which he is interested.*

Note that Mr. Rockefeller sets forth five essentials in a good solicitation: (1) The cause must be worthy, and you, the solicitor, must be informed. (2) You should know as much as possible about the person you are calling on. (3) You should give this person an idea as to the contributions others in his or her group are making. (4) You should suggest what you might like the prospect to give, leaving it to him or her to make the final decision. (5) You should be kindly and considerate: "Thus you will get closest to a man's heart and his pocketbook."

For the worker's kit in the Kingswood School campaign the section I prepared for the call in the home or office is shown in Form 20–2.

Note that both the Rockefeller piece and the Kingswood piece set forth the value of making a definite suggestion for the prospect to consider. Experienced fund raisers consider this to be the chief arrow in their quiver. More on this later.

The second arrow was brought home to me during a training session in Chicago for advance pledge workers. The dinner had been excellent, and the discussion on the WHY of the campaign, prior to my talk on techniques of solicitation, was so pertinent that I hesitated to cut off the talking. But time was speeding away, and I knew most of the workers had long drives home. Could I handle my instructions in a few minutes? What were the salient points— the irreducible minimum in successful calling? When I at length cut off the discussion, I stated: "The hour is late. You want to get home. But I must say something. If you forget everything else, there are two things you must remember about special fund raising. The barest essentials in this work are: first, make a dollar suggestion to each prospect; second, be ready to make a second call. The amount you suggest may require further thought by the prospect. Be willing, if you do not receive a favorable answer to your suggestion, to let the other person think it over. You will find that in the interval this suggestion is working for you. The prospect does not forget it. You may not get the full amount suggested, but you are apt to get more than if you quickly agreed on a smaller offer on your first visit."

KINGSWOOD NOW

To Our Workers:

We deeply appreciate your willingness to work for Kingswood in the "Kingswood Now" Program. This is a time of questioning in private education. Can the independent school survive in these days of spiralling costs? Can and will friends of private education provide the funds needed to keep private schools abreast of modern educational needs? We firmly believe not only that we can and will survive, but that we shall grow stronger. Much, of course, depends on this campaign, and on you the volunteer worker. Without your help, success is impossible.

The "Kingswood Now" Program is designed to provide a much-needed Science-Arts Building—by far the most ambitious building project in our history. Toward the anticipated cost of $2,250,000 we must now raise as much as possible. Long-range needs, to be faced sometime in the future, include additions to endowment, renovations in three houses and the Dining Hall, and improvements in the library and gymnasium.

Sincerely,

Robert A. Lazear

Robert A. Lazear
Headmaster

James B. Lyon

James B. Lyon '48
General Chairman

CULTIVATION

All of your prospects have some interest in Kingswood School. Many are Old Boys or parents—some are both. All of them have supported the School in some way.

Each of them knows something about the "Kingswood Now" Program because:

Each of them has received a letter with a copy of the "Kingswood Now" brochure.

Each is expecting a personal call.

PREPARATION

Your first and most important assignment is to decide what your *own* pledge will be. If it is generous, considering your circumstances and other commitments, you will be fully qualified to seek generous support from others.

Next, *read* thoughtfully the "Kingswood Now" brochure you will have been given so that you know the great value and importance of this campaign to Kingswood School.

Then reflect upon the *specific approach* you will make to each of your prospects. What will you suggest they consider as a pledge to Kingswood? Each of them will be looking to you for a suggestion. Have you studied the list of named gift opportunities? Some of these may appeal to your prospects.

You may wish someone to team up with you in your calling. If so, feel free to ask someone who, like you, will carry influence with your prospect. You may ask another worker or someone not yet recruited in our organization.

THE INTERVIEW

Please make *personal calls* on each of your prospects. Avoid telephone or mail solicitation. Take with you for your interview:

1. The prospect's pledge card.
2. This portfolio.
3. A copy of the "Kingswood Now" brochure.
4. Other materials, such as "Gifts This Year."

In most instances you know your prospects very well and can be friendly and comfortable in an interview. After you are settled, tell in your own words why the "Kingswood Now" Program is important, and why you are supporting it as generously as you can.

Be prepared to answer his questions, if you can. (See following pages.) If he has a question you cannot answer, obtain the answer and see him later.

Suggest some range of giving for his consideration. Show him the "Pattern of Giving" table. Whenever possible, talk about a specific facility which is needed. If he is interested, he will ask about the cost. In any event, emphasize what his gift will do, rather than the dollars he might wish to give.

If he is ready to make a decision, present his pledge card. If not, make an appointment to see him again. Do NOT LEAVE the pledge card.

A good interview requires a dedicated, thoughtful and enthusiastic solicitor who is willing to suggest a gift range and to help each of his prospects reach a decision.

QUESTIONS and ANSWERS

1. "Who Is Being Asked to Contribute?"

   All Old Boys, parents and friends of Kingswood School—wherever they may be located.

   *   *   *

2. "What Do You Suggest I Give?"

   We hope you will consider a named or memorial gift in the range of $ . . . ., payable at your convenience.

   *   *   *

3. "I Don't Believe in Pledges."

   Kingswood's needs cannot be met by "out-of-pocket" cash gifts. Would you consider a present gift and a review of your situation a year (or 3 months) from now?

   *   *   *

4. "May I Designate My Gift?"

   Certainly. Here is a list of named or memorial gifts in a very wide range. (See the brochure.)

   *   *   *

5. "May I Send in My Pledge Card?"

   I am responsible for the card and hope I may see you next week to let me know your decision. How about Tuesday for lunch again?

   *   *   *

6. "Why Does Kingswood Need a New Building?"

Kingswood's present enrollment is to be increased modestly to 425 boys for 1972. Even today's student body can no longer be accommodated in existing facilities. In addition to increased space, we need more adaptable space for modern educational needs.

7. "What Are These 'Space Needs?' "

In our gymnasium we have insufficient locker and shower space for today's enrollment. We can satisfy this need by converting the space now used by the drama department.

We have never had a music room. We are now sharing an all-purpose room in Nicholson building.

The art department meets in two modified basement rooms, crowded and poorly lighted. (See brochure for additional needs.)

* * *

8. "Is it Necessary to Tear Down the Second House on Campus?

The zoning hearing held by the town of West Hartford requires that we build on campus. A survey of many campus locations indicated that the most feasible spot was the location of the Science-Arts Building in place of the second house and the parking lot behind it. Our present playing fields and open space must be maintained as much as possible.

* * *

9. "What will the Science-Arts Building Include?"

Enlarged science laboratories, music practice and rehearsal rooms, drama-support rooms and stage and auditorium, fine arts and graphic arts rooms, a common room, and offices.

METHODS of GIVING

Budgeted Gifts: We trust that each of your prospects will be willing to make a pledge, payable over three years or more. Such budgeted giving will make it possible to reach our goal. It cannot be reached by out-of-pocket cash gifts. Should the donor be able to make a larger gift by taking more than three years to pay, encourage him to do so.

Gifts of Securities: Gifts of securities which have appreciated in value since their purchase are particularly advantageous to the donor. A savings on capital gains tax is possible, especially if paid in 1969. See your attorney or tax counselor for latest tax revisions.

For Gifts Involving Donative (Bargain) Sale, or Property, or Deferred Gifts: See your attorney or tax counselor for latest tax revision.

PLEDGE PAYMENT

We suggest payment within three years (four taxable years). Should anyone be able to make a larger gift by taking additional time, encourage him to do so, changing the pledge card accordingly. Also, if anyone states he is fully committed at present, suggest that he pledge now, with the first payment to be made whenever he wishes.

REMINDERS

1—YOUR SUCCESS in obtaining gifts for Kingswood will be determined largely by two factors:

– Your own financial commitment to this program.
– Your conviction and enthusiasm about Kingswood and its educational program.

2—PLEASE READ CAREFULLY all of the material given to you so that you are thoroughly familiar with the "Kingswood Now" Program.

3—SEE YOUR PROSPECTS PERSONALLY. Do not write. Do not telephone, except to make an appointment.

4—TAKE SUFFICIENT TIME to interest each prospect in the program *before* you discuss his participation. Do not give him his pledge card until he indicates he is ready to sign. In most cases, if you encourage him, he will tell you what his gift will be before he sees his card.

5—REPORT ALL PLEDGE CARDS. If you cannot see a prospect or obtain a pledge, record the facts on the reverse side of the prospect's card and return it.

6—DO NOT PROCRASTINATE. See your prospects immediately. Campaigns may fail—not because people fail to give—but because people are not called upon.

7—ANTICIPATE A FAVORABLE RESPONSE. Your prospects are interested in Kingswood School. They have supported it in the past. They will do so now.

MAKING THE APPOINTMENT

Calling on a major gift prospect generally requires an advance appointment. Telephoning ahead to the smaller gift prospect, on the other hand, often leads to a turndown or the comment: "Mail me the card." Phoning ahead calls for a certain persistence, a subtlety, that not everyone possesses. One must be prepared for a certain amount of stalling. One does not state over the phone that one is coming for a gift. Nor does one use subterfuge. It is wise to state that you represent a certain cause or organization, and wish to discuss a matter that will be of interest to the person called.

One should always work to get through to the principal. It is not good, in most cases, to put your cause before the prospect's secretary. Try to state your request for an appointment in terms of the advantage to the donor-to-be.

Sometimes you find it impossible to get through to the principal. Such was the case a few years ago with the former governor of Massachusetts—Alvin Fuller. We had been advised that it would be virtually impossible to see the governor: "He is the most difficult man in the state to get to see," stated one person. We would need to lay our case before his financial advisor. This we did—Edwin Tuller and I. Since the governor had been on the board twenty years earlier, we were hoping he would make a lead-off gift in a campaign to enlarge a home for the elderly. After Ed laid the case before the advisor, I said: "Our campaign is for $350,000. We need one gift of 10 percent. We hope the governor will give it."

The advisor's response was illuminating: "For many years I have been in charge of Mr. Fuller's giving. In all this time I have received hundreds of requests. Yours is the first one that suggested an amount. I like that, because you have made my job easier. I do not say how much you will get—or if you will get anything. But you have aided me by naming an amount."

It took us almost six months to get an answer. But then it came, partly as a result of the urging of his minister Hillyer Straton, a check for $25,000. The campaign resulted in an addition to the building somewhat larger than originally planned.

THE INTERVIEW

Length of Interview

Above all else the solicitor needs to treat the person called upon not as a prospect (I use the term in this book only as a matter of convenience), but as a person, an individual, perhaps a friend, certainly one who is concerned about improving the lot of humanity. How many callers forget this principle and open their conversation with the forbidden phrase: "I have come to get your gift." The least one can do is to make inquiry about matters of common interest.

The interview need not be long. One thirteen-minute solicitation resulted in a gift to an Ivy League university of not one, but two, gifts of a million dollars each.

A call was described to me by Louis Robey. He made the call accompanied by a college trustee, upon a benefactor who was far enough away to necessitate an overnight stay. This was in the days of World War II when travel was difficult to arrange. The two men were invited to be guests for dinner and overnight at the benefactor's home. They stayed up until midnight, discussing many matters, including the college, but not mentioning the hoped-for gift. Not until the end of the breakfast did they mention the amount desired. A few days later they received it. I have often wondered if I could have sat all evening without asking for the gift. Perhaps not. And perhaps I would have ruined the solicitation.

Suggesting the Amount Desired

When I told the leaders of the Covenant Presbyterian Church in Fort Myers, that we would rate the giving potential of members for their forthcoming campaign, I received opposition. This was not surprising, for it often happens in any group which has never rated. They believe that it is prying, and they fear criticism from those rated. Most of all, perhaps (and of course never voiced), is the reluctance of those present to have themselves rated. In brief, they are sure it will not work, at least not for their group. None of this bothered me. I knew that this step was the key to their raising the high goal they desired. What surprised me was the continued opposition to the idea.

Gradually we began making converts. The first group meeting—twenty-five leaders called together to do the initial rating—went well. A few present did not fill in dollar amounts as requested, but there was no outcry and the majority cooperated fully. Then came the review committee meeting. Those taking part began to see how the process was raising the sights of each one present. When the possibility of a high goal began emerging, higher than anyone had thought possible, some callers were willing to use the figure. Some, not all. The three or four using the suggested figure turned in pledges much higher than those not using it. Bob Rockwell, general chairman, now a convert, then went after other workers not yet believers. Their response: "These persons say they will be comfortable with what they are pledging," brought scorn from Bob. "It is not comfortable giving we need. It is sacrificial giving. It must be giving we will feel—not be comfortable with." Bob, and soon his top leadership, carried the day. The campaign raised $450,000 on a $400,000 goal, a goal thought to be impossible three weeks earlier. Here is how those members and friends pledged (over three years), above their giving to current expenses and benevolences:

PLEDGES TO COVENANT
PRESBYTERIAN CHURCH
MORTGAGE ELIMINATION

# of gifts		Amount	
1		$ 25,000	
1		20,000	
1		16,000	
1		15,600	
1		11,700	
1		10,500	
8		5,000 to 8,000	
5		4,000 to 4,900	
19		3,000 to 3,900	
3		2,500 to 2,900	
41	gave	240,640	53%
453	gave	210,579	47%
494	gave	$451,219	100%

A further breakdown of this church campaign, comparing ratings with results, reveals:

Rated at	Total calls	Number of pledges	Amount pledged	% of total pledged
A. $3,000 up	94	90	$287,603	64
B. 1,000–2,900	221	208	97,925	22
C. under 1,000	179	134	33,963	7
D. nonmembers	86	62	31,728	7
totals	580	494	451,219	100

You may have difficulty in persuading your group to rate their prospects, and then to use each individual's figure as a suggestion for his or her giving. But, if you win in selling this concept, you will raise a good deal more than otherwise.

How to present the suggested figure is important. If expressed wrongly, it could backfire. The figure to be presented to each is not a demand. You cannot insist on it. It is a suggestion only. But it is a suggestion that, fully understood, carries tremendous weight.

Many persons resent the idea of being "put down for something." Hence the question: "What do you have me down for?" is often a fighting question. Our invariable response is: "We do not have you down for anything. We are merely making a suggestion. You are free to accept or reject the figure."

An effective way to lead into the figure is to state in some detail how the figure was arrived at. Thus: "Two weeks ago twenty-three persons sat down together, each with a list of all friends (or members) before them. On the lists were names and addresses only. No financial information, or any other information. Each one worked alone. There was no talking, no comparison of figures. Each one asked a simple question. Not: "What *will* this person give?" But simply: "What *could* this person give?" Each began with his or her own name. Since there was no signing of names (every rating was confidential), the amount put down was not a pledge. It was an answer to the question: "What *could* I give if I became convinced of the worthiness of the project?" Each person then went to every name on the list they knew and put down a figure. Later a committee reviewed the averages, lowering some and raising a few. From the addition of these averages has come our goal. Thus we know that if everyone gives serious thought to one's own figure, our goal will be reached. There is a suggestion for everyone. There is a suggestion for you."

A most effective way for each visitor to introduce the suggested figure to each prospect is by repeating this story—how the rating was done—and then leaving the response up to the prospect.

Thousands of campaigns using this step have proven its value. It is a method calling for sensitivity and for understanding. When used properly, it works. How it works!

CALL BACKS

There are two occasions when the worker needs to consider a second call upon the prospect. The first is when the prospect asks for time to "think it over." This often happens, and there is no easy answer as to how to handle it, since each occasion is unique.

The request for additional time can be a stall, which may be based upon either unwillingness to give at all but reluctance to state an outright "no," or an unwillingness to give the amount stated. There are manuals on salesmanship which advise pressing ahead at this point for some decision, even though the amount will be less. Sensitivity and common sense (both of which are gifts of the gods) are called for here.

The second occasion is a legitimate inability to come to an immediate decision. Perhaps consultations need to be held with family, or attorney, or stock broker. These requests for delay should be honored graciously. They are usually to the advantage of the institution or cause. Sometimes the gift, when it comes, is more magnificent than the volunteer thought possible. The would-be donor, on the other hand, may not need counsel from others. He may merely need getting his own willingness up to the size of the gift suggested. Usually time is on the side of the seeker. The prospect may now have an inner struggle. His or her reflection becomes not: "Shall I give?," but rather: "How much shall I give?"

Related to this question of deciding whether to make a repeat call is another question: should one ever refuse a gift because of its small size? This situation, again, has no easy answer. It demands a gentle, nonjudgmental response. The turndown, hoping for a larger gift, should perhaps only be done by a friend of the giver, or by a top executive in the organization. A turndown must never be done haughtily or in a demeaning manner. And, if employed, expressed blame may be put upon the volunteer himself: "Mr. Jones, I have failed. I have been unsuccessful in showing you the tremendous importance of this cause. I would like to come back later after you have had time to rethink it."

There is one statement that can be made unequivocally. If

the caller uses tact in the refusal, and leaves the door open for a return visit, he or she will not lose the amount offered. On the second visit he or she will receive at least the amount offered, maybe more.

To the concerned prospect, who really desires to help, but is fearful of a pledge because of economic uncertainties, there is a way. It is the letter of intent. This written piece states that the signer intends or hopes to give a stated amount. Though it is unenforceable, it does have the power of a moral commitment. In some cases it will be as good as a signed pledge, and it is always better than no commitment at all.

The call on the prospect should be concluded as soon as the pledge is signed or the gift received. Salespersons sometimes "unsell" their customers by what happens after the order is signed. Since the purpose of your call is fulfilled when the commitment is made, you should thank the donor and leave immediately. One thing, however, remains. If there is a check or signed pledge, you should read aloud the amount to the giver. To do so avoids any misunderstanding of the amount, or of the intentions or conditions of the gift or giver. The contributor does not resent this. He or she knows you are going to look at the card or check as soon as you leave. So do it in his or her presence. And thank the donor again.

CHAPTER **21**

Step Fourteen:
Thanking the donor

The donor must be thanked. And he or she should be thanked quickly. In a large campaign, procedure must be thought out ahead of time and should be simplified to save much time.

When Booker T. Washington solicited funds to provide for Tuskegee Institute, he received in the mail one dollar from John D. Rockefeller. Washington duly thanked him. But he did more. At the end of the year he sent Rockefeller a detailed account of what he had done with the dollar. Impressed, Rockefeller now began to support his work in earnest.

We all liked to be thanked. In a sense, we demand it when it comes to philanthropy. Yet in the pressures of a capital drive, or in the hectic days of an annual drive, it is easy to overlook the daily thanking of donors. And thought must be given to types, or levels, of expressing thanks.

When the United Presbyterian Church in the U.S.A. was engaged in their Fifty Million Fund, we had a score or so of area counselors stationed across the nation. One day I arrived at the office of Charles McCloskey, counselor in Illinois. "Here is some good news," he said. "This came by mail, entirely unsolicited." He showed me a check for $10,000. "What are you doing about it?" I inquired. "Oh, I shall send the donor a personal thank you."

A couple of weeks later when I returned, Chuck showed me a second check for $10,000. "This came after the giver received

162

my 'thank you.' " "Have you," I asked, "thanked him?" "The letter is now in the typewriter," he responded.

On my third visit Chuck was ecstatic: "Another check for $10,000 arrived this morning." "And what will you do?" "I'll send another letter," said Chuck. "No. Not this time. Now you must go in person to thank him."

Chuck went and expressed gratitude. The manufacturer who had made the gift responded: "Business has been good this year. I am glad to share." He reached for his checkbook and handed over a fourth check for another $10,000. This experience was the beginning of Chuck's record of highest over-subscription of goals in the nation—180 percent of his goal.

It is essential that you plan ahead as to how you will send out acknowledgment of gifts. This important step cannot be left to happenstance. Most groups will need to assign one (or more) person(s) to this task and aim for mailing the receipt not later than twenty-four hours after receiving the gift.

In several of my campaigns we printed up forms that were warmer than the receipts purchased at any stationers. Form 21–1 is the one we used for the YW. It is a card folded to 4 x 5 size, with matching envelope. The inside is completely blank so that the YW had flexibility in its wording. These were mailed out with typed messages inside ranging from a simple: "$50" to wording as personal and elaborate as desired.

Form 21–1

THE BOARD OF DIRECTORS

of the

YWCA of the HARTFORD REGION, INC.

GRATEFULLY ACKNOWLEDGE RECEIPT

OF YOUR GIFT

TO THE

BUILDING CAMPAIGN

Forms should not be used in thanking trustees, past trustees, and special donors. These call for personal letters from the chief executive.

Larger gifts, as in a capital campaign, call for more than a letter. A letter, including an invitation to luncheon, would be an appropriate way to thank the sender of a larger than average gift. Complimentary tickets to some affair your society is promoting would be in order for a few larger donors. As the gift gets into the very top category, you may wish to arrange a small dinner party as your way of showing appreciation.

Publicity given to larger gifts is often employed. If the gift is significant, the donor may agree to newspaper or television coverage. Listing of givers in your organization's publicity pieces is a time-honored way that should not be overlooked. Think of such publicity as of twofold purpose: to thank the giver and to encourage others to give. When do you need to obtain permission to print names of donors in your own periodicals? Practically never. We all like to see our names in print, particularly in association with our peers.

It is standard campaign practice to print names of donors in the organization's publicity pieces, beginning with a small list in the early phase and continuing from time to time with an ever expanding list. These listings are most valuable when set up in categories of gifts. Thus your top listing would be givers of the very highest amounts, other categories of decreasing amounts, until the largest grouping at the bottom with the smallest gifts. Sometimes the actual dollar amount is stated. More often it is not. Generally a name is given to each category, such as "benefactors" for the few large gifts, "supporters" for the intermediate gifts, and "general givers" for the smaller gifts. Publicity is sent out early in the drive announcing these categories, and placing a dollar value on each. In a capital drive, the listing of names may begin with a stated minimum gift. The campaign states that all giving at least this minimum amount will be published in a forthcoming issue.

As the YWCA campaign began receiving early pledges, we sensed it was time to print our first listing of supporters. Our top category was a group of nine gifts beginning with $10,000. There were, of course, many more contributors of lesser amounts. Though I had never received a complaint on publishing donors' names, this time I was determined to run an experiment in which I would ask permission to use names. I called the top nine givers, stating what I had in mind. When I explained that the main purpose was to encourage others to become contributors, rather than to give prominence to the givers, seven gave permission while the other two said they preferred being listed as anonymous. I did not ask any other person for permission. When printed, there were almost one hundred names. Not a single person complained.

Some campaigns announce ahead of time that a bronze plaque will be placed on the inside wall giving names of all who contribute a certain minimum. This strategy is an effective producer. Think of your hometown. Who would not like to have his or her name on the walls of Metropolitan Opera in Lincoln Center, or the Museum of Fine Arts in Boston, or a library, museum, or school in your town?

CHAPTER 22

Step Fifteen:
Cleaning up and collecting

There are many loose ends to be tied up when the drive officially ends. These items range from additional funds obtained by completing every call to long-range benefits obtained by such office procedures as proper record-keeping.

The telephone rang while I was preparing this chapter. The secretary of the church campaign I had finished directing three months ago was calling. I had left at the time when they had subscribed $151,000 on a goal of $150,000. "We now have $162,000 pledged," she stated, "and I'm sure we shall go to $170,000." After the drive "officially" closed, an additional $11,000 plus another expected $8,000—13 percent over goal.

Such a result is a tribute to the efficient work of Ethel Cole of Northboro, Massachusetts, and her committee. Yet it is not at all unusual. The flow of new money need not stop when the campaign closes. But the flow generally happens only when the organization is alert and attends to follow-up.

COMPLETING THE CALLING

Let's look at the loose ends. They comprise:

– calls never assigned to anyone
– calls assigned, but no contact made due to unavailability of prospect

– contact made, but additional time requested
– calls assigned but worker unable to complete because of own illness, busy schedule, or laziness
– follow-up calls when donor says: "I will give more later."
– and, in rare cases, repeat calls on a few who refused but may reconsider.

The usual way to handle incomplete calls is to give those workers who desire, an extra ten days. Do not let them hold cards that cannot be completed (because prospect is at present unavailable) for three weeks or more. Forgetfulness, coupled with dying enthusiasm, is too great a hurdle to get over.

The clean-up of calls must be handed over to a select group of volunteers who proved themselves during the active campaign. Select these workers ONLY on the basis of production in their calling. Let them know why they were selected and who else will work with them. The eliteness of this group appeals to them.

Before they gather, someone needs to make a thorough study of the calls to be made. Some of these pledge cards (or prospect cards) will be lost. Some will be dirty or torn. Others will need change of name or address. After you have this revised pack of cards, you will want to group them by category of giving. You may want to rerate a few. Finally, it is wise to make a new master list for these remaining cards. See Form 22–1.

Then get your flying squad together. Take a few minutes to announce latest dollar returns (use a few names with amounts), state how many cards need a recall, and how much is expected from these remaining cards. Set a time and place for reporting. Build it around a complimentary meal at a convenient place.

Form 22–1

YWCA of the Hartford Region, Inc.

New Building Prospect Master List — 1970-1971

CATEGORY _____ PAGE _____ OF _____ PAGES

NO.	PROSPECT	SOLICITOR	RATING	RESULTS	COMMENTS

This Form 22–1 is a reduction from original 11″ × 14″ size. If reproduced, restore to original size.

RECORDING GIFTS

Everyone agrees that good records should be kept of all gifts. Yet many organizations, even those in existence a long time, can be very dilatory. Good records not only are the basis of sound public relations, not only are the cornerstone of keeping shrinkage to a minimum, but are also the beginning of your next drive. Do not be one of those institutions which believe (they are never quite sure) that the records of the last campaign may be up in the attic under that pile of books discarded by the former librarian.

If you used a master list in your drive, complete it now by entering all amounts given, or pledges made. Enter also any notations such as: "See after July fifteen."

Keep a permanent card file, in addition to the current pledge or cash card. The reason is that some persons do not give to the present drive, but have given before and will give again. So set up a card system for a ten year record of giving—for annual, for capital, and for bequests. The 3 x 5 card is far too small. Make it least 4 x 6. (Harvard University's card is 8 x 10.) It has to be a card so that new additions can always be kept alphabetical. Form 22–2 was the permanent record card we made for Kingswood School in the 1960s.

If your donors are paying on a pledge (usually three years) or are making several payments in a year, you will need a payment card. Form 22–3 is the card designed for recording payments to the Hartford YWCA capital campaign.

Form 22–2

	CAPITAL GIVING
	1955 $ _____
	1961 $ _____
	1969 $ _____
(BUSINESS) (POSITION)	ANNUAL GIVING
(STREET ADDRESS)	
(CITY) (STATE) (ZIP)	62 _____ 69 _____
	63 _____ 70 _____
Sons at Kingswood Grandsons at Kingswood	64 _____ 71 _____
	65 _____ 72 _____
	66 _____ 73 _____
	67 _____ 74 _____
	68 _____ 75 _____

Form 22–3

	YWCA CAPITAL GIFTS

PLEDGE CARD NO. _____

DATE	PLEDGED		PAID		BALANCE DUE	RESTRICTION
	$	CUMULATIVE	$	CUMULATIVE	$	

Will your group be receiving many payments in a brief period, or quite a few each week for a year or more? Then you will need a daily transmittal sheet. Contributions or pledges are entered by date by the person who opens the mail. Often three copies are made—one for the president, one for the bookkeeper or treasurer, and one for the development director. This sheet allows you to keep abreast of two totals: (1) total for the day or week, and (2) cumulative total. Sheet A is to record pledges in a capital campaign. See Form 22–4 for Kingswood's transmittal A. Sheet B is to record only cash payments, by date as received. See Form 22–5. These transmittal sheets, needed for larger campaigns, are not a substitute for the permanent record card, which is an alphabetical file.

A prospect list is only as good as the address on it. Make sure that one person is responsible for all address changes, which is to be done after each mailing, and particularly after each campaign or solicitation.

There may be special requests made by donors at time of giving. Record these, where appropriate, on the individual record card. Make sure that all concerned staff, or faculty, are notified.

Full records of giving, easily accessible, will make your next drive much simpler. That may seem like a long way off, and you

Form 22–4

"KINGSWOOD NOW" CAPITAL PROGRAM

LISTING OF PLEDGES

DAILY TRANSMITTAL SHEET A

SHEET NO. _____

DATE _____

NO	NAME	DOLLARS	CENTS	CHECK WHEN THANKED	CATEGORY	RESTRICTIONS
	BALANCE FORWARD					
	TOTAL TO DATE					

Form 22–4 has been reduced from original size of 8½″ × 11″

Form 22–5

"KINGSWOOD NOW" CAPITAL PROGRAM

PAYMENTS ON PLEDGES (CASH RECEIPTS)

DAILY TRANSMITTAL SHEET B

SHEET NO _____

DATE _____

NO.	NAME	DOLLARS	CENTS	RESTRICTIONS
	BALANCE FORWARD			
	TOTAL TO DATE			

Form 22–5 has been reduced from original size of 8½" × 11"

may feel exhausted by the drive now ending, but some day you, or your successor, will rise up and call you blessed.

COLLECTING YOUR PLEDGES

It is human to forget. The pledger means to pay, but often needs reminding. This is particularly so if he or she elects to pay quarterly and essential if annually. When the pledger is reminded courteously, he or she will not consider it a dunning, but will be grateful. Printed forms can be made up, to be filled in with name, address, amount of original pledge, amount paid to date, and amount due. Be careful with that last item. It not only must be accurate and up to date (did the check arrive a week ago on someone else's desk and you have not yet been notified?). It must be gently worded, for assuredly this is not a bill from the telephone or electric company. Sometimes it might be good public relations not to fill in the line for amount due, relying on the recipient to do his or her own figuring.

Most pledge cards in capital campaigns are made up as legal documents (the phrase "in consideration of the gifts of others" takes care of this). But the day has passed when institutions sue to collect pledges. Such action is extremely injurious to the image of the institution. This legal card does carry moral weight with the donor and may be of benefit in collecting any unpaid portion from a deceased person's estate. Even here, great delicacy must be the guide in determining whether to approach the administrator of the estate.

In addition to enclosing an addressed envelope, this envelope sometimes is a return-postage paid envelope with permit number. It is not considered essential to provide the actual stamp for the envelope.

CHAPTER **23**

Step Sixteen:
Reporting results

The preparing of a final report for each drive is a discipline that will enable trustees and administration to see the picture as a whole—the statistics of the drive, unfinished elements, guidelines for final collection of funds, and recommendations for future action.

Every drive for funds, regardless of scope and amount, should culminate in a final written report. The head fund raiser carries much of the campaign in his or her head, and owes it to the trustees to reduce this experience to written form. The very doing so will be an asset as he or she seeks to profit from mistakes and omissions and especially in planning future steps. The time to do so is while the fund raiser is still battle weary. Facts and statistics are still fresh and easily recallable. Delay leads to postponement, and too often to no report at all.

ELEMENTS OF FINAL REPORT
Analysis of Campaign
Statistics—The Tangibles

This should be a greatly condensed summary dealing with statistics. It can often be written on one sheet of paper. The items to be listed include:

- date and name of drive
- total number of prospects

- total number of mailings
- number of prospects called on personally
- number of prospects who gave
- number of prospects who refused
- number of prospects not reached
- number of callers
- amount received by mail
- amount received by visitations
- amount received by other means
- amount received from individuals
- amount received from foundations
- amount received from corporations
- amount received from government grants
- amount received from trustees
- total cash
- total cash and pledges

Further items could be:

- number of members (or alumni)
    number who gave and amount
- number of nonmembers (or nonalumni)
    number who gave and amount
- number of nonresidents
    number who gave and amount

Overview—The Nontangibles

The positive achievements of the drive should be listed with editorial comments. There are usually some trustees, or administration, who do not realize the import of the campaign. Everyone likes to see large numbers of dollars reported, especially when the goal is over-subscribed or when last year's figure is surpassed. That is not, how-ever, the sole advantage of the fund-raising effort. Often it is the lesser good. For a well-run campaign results in many intangibles. Included among these are such elements as forcing the organization to reconsider its program and then to tell its story to the public, the heightened awareness of the public, the opening of the way for bequests and other deferred gifts, and the renewed dedication of staff and trustees. Setting forth these nonsubstantive gains will help all to "see life steadily and see it whole."

Weaknesses and Omissions

All drives have weaknesses and omissions, and always will. Campaigning is too much of a human adventure for it to be otherwise. Every year—every cause—has its changes. Aims, purposes, programs change. It is not a sign of weakness to admit to omissions or unproductive steps but rather a sign of strength or leadership. The recording of such reflections will assist future efforts in fund raising.

Immediate Steps

Loose Ends

There are always loose ends to be taken care of—calls yet to be made, scores of telephone calls to be made, perhaps even a new printed piece to be prepared. It would be helpful to set forth these tasks in this final report. See Chapter Twenty-one again.

New Avenues to Explore

Less immediate would be tasks in areas not yet begun. Perhaps you campaigned in one or two major centers. Are there other cities or districts you might now move into with more leisurely pace? Are there personal interviews you might now have with corporations or individuals that could be productive in the long view rather than immediately? Are there feature stories that you were unable to prepare earlier because of pressure of time? Perhaps the campaign opened new vistas to you and your leaders—avenues suggested by the campaign which you were unable to explore at the time. List these in your final report. The distribution of your statement may bring forth new volunteers to help achieve these ideas. A year from now you (or your successor) may be grateful for this written record.

Collecting of Funds

The final report should outline steps to ensure the collection of promised funds. Perhaps your organization has a complete system. It might be helpful to review it here in barest outline, since there may be readers who could offer improvements. If your organization is new, or your fund raising has not had years of experience, your report should contain a section on steps to be followed.

The simplest setting forth of a collection system involves:

- determining responsibility—staff. Is this to be staff responsibility? If so, do not give it to the treasurer or bookkeeper. This sensitive step belongs to the development office.
- determining responsibility—volunteers. Is your organization in a position to use volunteers? Then name a committee to oversee collections.

Have them meet regularly and report to the trustees. Give them a small budget.

– use of efficient office procedures. Review Chapter Twenty-one for suggested forms. If your organization is large, obtain information from specialists in the field. New helps are being developed annually, and information is usually free from salespersons or from users of the system in other institutions.

These steps—and others—can be recommended in the final report.

Recommendations for Future Action

By the time the drive ends, the development director knows more about current fund raising than anyone else in the organization. He or she may not have had opportunity—or time—to share his or her conclusions with those who direct the institution or cause. Let the director now set forth these thoughts as recommendations in his or her final report.

When I assisted the Pacific School of Religion in a drive, it became evident to me that the one-man development office was vastly undermanned, particularly since there was no president to handle many of the duties now resting upon the development office. The combination of having no president and an over-burdened development office greatly delayed the securing of funds. In my final report I recommended enlarging the staff. Eighteen months later, after inauguration of a president and tripling of size of the development office, the building funds were oversubscribed.

The writer of the final report may wish to recommend engaging part-time professional counsel in fund raising, or part-time writing assistance, or additional staff, or greater funds for publicity. Most of all, the writer can summarize his or her thinking on new out-reaches—untried ways to reach a greater public. He or she can advocate the holding of events that directly raise no funds but indirectly do through increasing the number of friends and concerned persons. This person can promote the idea of the staff opening their homes for social gatherings of supporters, and of trustees assuming responsibilities of cultivating potential donors, personally assigned to the trustee. He or she can push for the holding of events to attract donors—open house or a conference, a concert or a series of small dinners for the select.

The final report, carefully written, can be a vehicle for advancing many ideas.

Form 23–1 gives the statistical part of a final report to a church.

176

Form 23–1

REPORT TO THE STEPS IN RENEWAL CAMPAIGN COMMITTEE

FIRST BAPTIST CHURCH
WEST HARTFORD, CT

ANALYSIS OF CAMPAIGN

Number of pledge cards:
  180 white cards (resident, general members)
  36 blue cards (advance pledges)
  __23 green cards (nonmembers)
  239
  __35 mail cards
  274 total

GOALS

Basic—$125,000
Victory—$145,000
Challenge—$165,000

Number of Cards		Dollars pledged
Reported in:	Outstanding:	
April 20–187	52	$132,601
April 23–204	35	151,393
May 10–224	15	161,916

Of the 187 cards reported by April 20, the results are:

	White	Blue	Green	Total
Number of pledges	100	26	11	137
Number of refusals	46	0	4	50

Category of Pledges

		Cards	Amount
1.	Advance	26	$ 55,800
2.	Regular	95	68,893
3.	Friends	11	5,495
4.	Nonresidents	2	263
5.	Nursery School Committee	1	1,000
6.	David Crockett Memorial	1	650
7.	Chinese Fellowship	1	500
		137	$132,601

Cash received—April 23—$16,622
Note: Final pledged amount was $161,916.

CHAPTER 24

Looking to foundations, corporations, and government

In 1979 foundations in America gave over two billion dollars to philanthropy. Corporations in 1979, for the first time, surpassed this amount. Both continue to grow year by year. Yet requests far exceed funds available. Can you expect to share in this distribution? How do you go about it?

The main source of private philanthropic giving in America has always been the individual. In 1978 the individual donor contributed 89½ percent of the entire philanthropic dollar, whereas 5½ percent came from foundations, and 5 percent from corporations. The main thrust of this book is directed at personal giving. But keep in mind that some smaller corporations and family foundations are also approached as individuals.

Foundations, corporations, and government grants cannot, assuredly, be overlooked. In 1979 foundations in America gave away $2.24 billion. Corporations added another $2.3 billion.

FOUNDATIONS

The *Foundation Directory*, seventh edition, states that there are 21,505 active grant-making foundations in the country. Most of these have rather small assets. The larger ones, 3,138 listed in the directory, comprise 93 percent of assets of all U.S. foundations and account for 92 percent of all grants.

With all these funds available, and with all the publicity that is given these gifts, it is no wonder that young fund raisers feel here is a bonanza, the answer to prayer of all fund-seeking organizations.

Yet for every institution or cause that obtains a foundation gift, there are many more that are refused. Here is the record of seven foundations for a recent twelve month period:

	# of requests	# of grants
Ford	20,000	2,150
Robert W. Johnson	1,400	148
W. K. Kellogg	3,302	164
Kresge	1,190	177
Rockefeller Brothers	2,081	166
Totals	27,973	2,805 or 10%

Community foundations appear to have a much higher ratio of acceptances. Here are two:

Permanent Charity Fund (Boston)	318	125
The Cleveland Foundation	570	322
Totals	888	447 or 50%

In submitting these figures, Mariam C. Noland of the Cleveland Foundation writes:

"Let me strongly point out that, from the standpoint of a community foundation, the statistic in relation to the number of requests to grants made is not particularly meaningful. We are, in fact, able to meet the majority of requests that are realistic and of high quality. The constraint of dollars is in many cases not as significant as the availability of high quality applications and persons who can carry those activities out."*

The ratio of acceptances among larger foundations being about one in ten would indicate that most applicants will be disappointed.

* Mariam C. Noland, Program Officer, The Cleveland Foundation.

Someone, of course, is going to receive those grants. So here are some guides.

Types of Foundations and Fields of Interest

There are five general kinds of foundations:

1. General purpose. The largest and best known. Interested in a wide spread of projects.
2. Special purpose. Restricted to a geographical area or a specific field of interest.
3. Corporate. Established by companies or corporations to handle funds donated by the company. May be restricted to location of main office.
4. Family. Usually small in assets. Under control of family which set them up. Often are not included in any listing.
5. Community. Many small funds centralized under community management. Grants usually restricted to local area.

The fields of interest of most foundations, particularly the larger ones, can be classified as health, education, religion, science, welfare, humanitarian needs, and international causes. Donors, especially to family foundations, may set up their funds to reflect other interests.

Getting Started with Foundations

The Foundation Center (888 Seventh Avenue, New York, N.Y., 10019) was established to bring together all pertinent information on foundations in America and to aid in disseminating such information. They do not assist in approaching foundations but are invaluable in providing many services and publications. The center has branch offices in Washington, Cleveland, and San Francisco. The offices in New York and Washington contain the IRS returns (990-PK and 990-AR) for all private foundations in the U.S. The Cleveland and San Francisco offices contain the IRS records for those foundations in the middle and western sections of the country. In addition the center sponsors cooperating collections in all fifty states plus Puerto Rico, Virgin Islands, and Mexico City. These cooperating collections usually contain IRS records only for foundations within their states. Many foundation annual reports are kept in these libraries.

The center's opus magnum is *The Foundation Directory*, revised every few years and found in most public libraries. The directory lists names and addresses by states of almost 3,200 foundations, gives the purpose and activities, sets forth financial figures such as assets and expenditures, and lists names of officers and trustees. It is an absolute must as a reference work. Other publications of the center are the *National Data Book*, giving brief descriptions of over 26,000 foundations, *Source Book Profiles* (a loose-leaf subscription service with in-depth analyses of 1,000 major foundations), *Foundation Grants to Individuals,* describing over 1,000 foundations making grants to individuals, and *Foundation Grants Index*, an annual index to over 15,000 grants. The Council on Foundations (1828 L Street, N.W., Washington, D.C., 20036), works closely with the Foundation Center and publishes *Foundation News,* a bimonthly which contains the *Foundation Grants Index.* The current listings are cumulative, and form the *Foundation Grants Index* of the Foundation Center for the next year.

In seeking foundation support, the beginner should first turn to the *Index of Fields of Interest* at the back of the directory. Then survey the foundations listed under the state in which you are interested. A good guide to finding grant sources and writing grant proposals is Robert Lefferts: *Getting a Grant,* Prentice-Hall, Inc., Englewood Cliffs, New Jersey, 07632.

There are many state directories published such as the *Directory of Foundations in Massachusetts,* compiled by the Division of Public Charities, Office of Attorney General of Massachusetts.

Much homework on your part is essential prior to approaching any foundation. Using various directories, you will narrow your search to perhaps half a dozen foundations that make grants in your field and your geographical location. Most foundations publish an annual report which is available for the asking. Their listing of recent grants provides a guide to their current thinking.

The next step in seeking foundation support is to try for an interview with the executive officer. Use the telephone, though this is sometimes difficult to pull off. Many foundations insist on a written proposal before the interview. You, however, may not be ready for writing your proposal. First you want to sound out the officers. What do they like? How go about it? What are deadlines?

Perhaps one of your directors knows a foundation trustee. By all means sound the trustee out for advice, and see if he or she can set up an appointment with the staff. Do not take an end-run-around staff. They will resent it.

It is better not to leave a proposal at your interview, nor to name a dollar figure. The direction of your proposal and the requested amount can be decided on later. The development officer of one of my clients told me that $100,000 was being requested from a large foundation. "How," I asked, "did you arrive at that figure?" "Oh, it is an educated guess." "I suggest," I replied, "that since you know the foundation's executive officer you ask him how much to ask for at this time." The reply came back: "Try for $75,000." They did, and eventually got it.

Writing the Proposal

John Kerr, in his course at Harvard University's Center for Lifelong Learning, lists nine items to be included in a written proposal:

1. introduction
2. amount requested
3. the problem you are attempting to solve
4. background of your institution or cause—previous accomplishments
5. your plan and schedule in raising funds to accomplish objectives of your institution
6. names of persons involved
7. budget, including cost ratio
8. method of evaluating results
9. how you will finance after the grant ends

The Kresge Foundation prints some guidelines that you should find helpful in approaching any large foundation:

Form 24–1

POLICIES AND APPLICATION PROCEDURES

Who may apply?

Well-established, financially sound, fully accredited, tax-exempt organizations operating in the fields of (a) four-year college and university education, (b) health care and related services, (c) social welfare, (d) conservation, (e) the arts and humanities, and (f) care of the young and old.

For what purposes?

Only toward projects involving (a) construction of facilities, (b) renovation of facilities, (c) purchase of major movable equipment having

---

a unit cost of not less than $50,000, and (d) the purchase of real estate.

Requests toward debt retirement or completed projects will not be accepted.

Are application forms used?

The Foundation does not use application forms. *The information which must be included in applications is listed on pages 4 and 5.* Incomplete applications will delay the review process.

When are applications accepted?

Applications will be accepted **only** during the period beginning January 1 and ending March 31 of each year. Significant changes or developments should be reported as soon as they occur.

All applications are reviewed with the same standard of care. However, a submission early in the application period (if the option exists) will help us utilize our review procedures in a more timely fashion.

When will decisions be announced?

Favorable decisions are announced about mid-July. Most declinations are announced prior to that date, although we must warn applicants that some declination notices could be received as late as one week before grant announcements.

How does the Foundation make grants?

The Foundation does not generally grant initial funds or total project costs. Grants are usually made on a challenge basis. Typically, the successful applicant has already raised some money, and a grant is then made for a portion of the remaining funds. The challenge involved is not based on any specific or matching formula, but rather requires the raising of the remaining funds, thereby insuring completion of a project.

Payment of a challenge grant is normally conditioned upon:

(a) raising the balance of the funds required by a certain date and
(b) notification of the actual project contract price and assurance that it is within available resources.

Can appointments be made?

While visits to the Foundation offices are not required, every effort will be made to honor such requests throughout the year. If should be understood that appointments do not insure subsequent grant commitments. Furthermore, grants are made to many organizations which do not meet with us.

What about future requests?

Organizations which have previously received a grant commitment may apply toward a different project provided the payment conditions of any prior grant have been fully satisfied.

If the Foundation has declined a request, the applicant may reapply in a subsequent application period. Requests may be for the same project, provided it remains eligible, or for another project. Such applications should be complete in all respects without reliance upon previously submitted information.

What about other questions?

Additional information can be found in our current Annual Report which is available upon request. Written or telephone inquiries can be made.

AN APPLICATION MUST CONTAIN
THE FOLLOWING INFORMATION

ABOUT THE PROJECT

- A brief covering letter, signed by a fully authorized official, which clearly describes the project, its purpose, and priority for the institution.
- The actual or estimated date of any required local or governmental approval (Certificate of Need, zoning, etc.).
- Project commencement and completion dates (month and year for each).

- Actual or estimated total project cost. Identify principal components such as construction, equipment, furnishings, fees, etc.
- A listing, by principal sources, of all funds presently on hand or formally pledged. Explain fully all present or anticipated financing.
- Amount requested.
- Proposed method of raising the remaining funds and fund raising timetable.
- The estimated annual operating and maintenance costs (utilities, etc.) of the completed project, the basis of determining these costs, and the plan for covering these costs in the organization's operating budget. If a special operating endowment is planned, specify this endowment goal and amount presently raised toward the goal.
- A small photograph or drawing of the project. Do not furnish blueprints.

ABOUT THE INSTITUTION

- A fact sheet summarizing significant use statistics about the applying institution with comparable data for the current and prior two years (membership, full time equivalent enrollment, number of beds and percent of occupancy, etc.).
- The status of each accreditation held, and affiliation with any other organization.
- Reasonable assurances of present and future organizational financial stability. Include a summary statement of the actual operating income and expenses for each of the last three fiscal years and budgetary projections for the current and following years.
- One complete copy of the most recent audited financial reports.
- An explanation of the reason(s) for any deficits and a listing of specific sources used to cover such deficits.
- Current market value of endowment, if any.
- A brief description of the plan for operating and maintaining the organization's present physical plant. Give the percentage of the operating budget devoted to this and the amount designated annually for major repair, replacement or funded depreciation.

> • The Internal Revenue Service determination letter proving that the applicant is (1) a tax-exempt, charitable organization and (2) is not classified as a private foundation within the meaning of Section 509 of the Internal Revenue Code.

CORPORATIONS

Corporations in America give away but 1 percent of their pre-tax earnings (profits, not sales). Law allows them to donate 5 percent of profits before taxes. Although total dollars given does increase yearly, the percentage of profits given remains within a narrow range of 1 to 1¼ percent. In 1970, reported the Commission on Private Philanthropy in 1975, the tax returns of 1.7 million corporations showed only 20 percent of them giving to charitable causes, and only 6 percent giving over $500 for the year. Corporate giving is on the upward swing. By 1979 about 30 percent of American corporations were contributing regularly to philanthropy, reported The Conference Board. The main recipients of corporate support are education, health and welfare, and federated drives. Some corporations will give to colleges and universities, often in exchange for research or special courses. Gifts in kind are not unusual, accompanied now and then by cash to keep up the equipment.

There are two avenues to corporation gifts. The usual one is through a committee set up by the company to disburse funds given to the corporation foundation. In a smaller size company the chief disburser may be the president. In a larger company it could be a vice-president or perhaps the public relations committee. Since the amount set aside annually is severely limited, each individual gift will be limited. Even for a large corporation, a gift of $10,000 might be considered quite large.

Find out which companies have set up a procedure on gifts, then inquire as to who is chairperson. Next obtain a list of gifts made during the past three years. From there on the process is the same as approaching an individual, though the corporate gift may require many weeks to be voted.

The other way is to be used only when you have a director who has access to the firm's president or chairperson, or your cause is so localized and advantageous to community and company that direct action by the board is justified. This approach was used by both the YMCA and the YWCA of Hartford, Connecticut, in two separate building campaigns. The YW secured gifts of $400,000, $250,000, $200,000, and $100,000 from four insurance companies, $300,000 from one industry, and $75,000 each from two banks. One of the appeals to these businesses was that the YW would provide moderately priced housing for young working women. Another reason for these significant gifts was the chairperson for the YW drive—James Stewart, Senior Vice-President of Travelers Insurance Company, who was an indefatigable advocate.

Corporate gifts are not easy to obtain. Set your sights high, but be practical. The after-tax profit of the average corporation is only slightly over 6 percent of their total sales. Most larger companies today have professionally trained managers, responsible to others: their bosses, stockholders, and even their employees. These managers must make a profit or they fail and their business fails. Therefore, make it as easy as possible for them. Show how your cause is not only good, but good also for the company's short- or long-range best interests.

GOVERNMENT GRANTS

Government grants in the fields of education, health, science, welfare, and the arts is 100 or more times greater than foundation grants, declares the Foundation Center of New York.

The obtaining of government grants is a complicated, often frustrating, experience. There are many counselors in the country who specialize in guiding nonprofit institutions in obtaining such funding. They earn their fees in this labyrinth.

Lest anyone think that government grants are a pure handout, consider the study made by the General Accounting Office of grants made in 1976 by the Office of Environmental Education of the Department of Health, Education, and Welfare. The office made ninety grants totaling $3 million. Applications filed were 1,154, at a preparation cost to the institutions of $1.2 million. That is about $1,000 an application, or 40 percent of the entire grant.

Perhaps your city has funds available. Such a source was greatly enriched by Congress's passing of the Revenue Sharing plan. Call the mayor's office to see what division of the city government handles funds for education or philanthropy. Request any printed guidelines.

There are many governmental newsletters available, most of them free of charge. They do not, however, give information on grants but provide background or feature stories. Examples are *Cultural Post* from the National Endowment for the Arts and *Humani-*

ties from the National Endowment for the Humanities. Other newsletters are distributed by the Office of Education (for a charge), Community Services Administration, and Health Resources Administration.

If all this leaves your head spinning, you might drop in for a chat and an armful of free literature from your regional office of the U.S. Department of Health, Education, and Welfare, now called the Department of Health and Human Services.

CHAPTER 25

Planned giving, annuities, and bequests

A growing trend in fund raising is the deferred gift. This may be a transfer of money or property to a trust fund that pays the donor a lifetime annuity. Or it may be a bequest. There are a variety of trusts from which to choose.

Institutions in America are becoming increasingly aware of the fund-raising potential in the deferred gift, which can be either through bequest or a trust providing life income to the donor. Harvard University prefers calling this program "Planned Giving." Michael Boland, the university's director of planned giving, believes that charitable trusts are growing by at least 20 percent per year. All "planned" gifts are not large. More than 50 percent of Harvard's pooled income funds are in the range of $5,000 to $10,000. One advantage of these smaller gifts is that there are many repeat gifts—as high as 40 percent, reports Boland. An often overlooked aspect is that most very large gifts are designated for specific causes. When the institution presses unduly for unrestricted giving, it is failing to take the donor's point of view.

One reason for this growing popularity of planned giving is the number of potential donors who are not in an economic position to make sizable gifts now, since they need their money for retirement living. Philanthropic institutions have come to the realization that they have been missing many gifts which, through planned giving, could eventually come their way from persons who are non-givers, or at least, modest givers. A helpful change in handling such funds has been brought about by a number of national banks, investment houses, and even law firms, which have recently set up pooled income funds. For a nominal management fee (½ to 1 percent of assets) these agents will accept deposits of as small as $1,000, which they place into one pooled investment fund. The donors are then paid by the bank, at stated periods, the earnings which are lifelong.

Planned giving occurs almost entirely where the fund-seeking organization has given some person, staff or volunteer, responsibility for promotion. Pamphlets must be prepared and distributed periodically. There are firms in America which supply these, ready printed, to an institution. Publicity should be given to the program and to participants.

LIFE-INCOME PLANS

Life-income trusts offer many advantages to the donor. They avoid any capital gains tax on appreciated securities. They give a charitable income tax deduction. They reduce or avoid estate taxes. There is no charge for advice given by the receiving institution. Often they present a stepped-up annual yield to the donor.

There are several ways one may make a gift to a charitable or educational organization and receive a lifetime income from earnings. These plans are:

- annuity trust
- unitrust
- pooled income
- gift annuity
- deferred payment gift annuity
- life estates

Charitable Remainder Annuity Trust

This income plan is set up by transferring assets to a trust fund which pays during one's lifetime a fixed dollar amount annually. Benefits can also be paid to a survivor. The trust principal, of course, belongs to the philanthropic institution. The donor receives a guaranteed return. Should the trust not earn that much in any one year, the trustee pays the difference from principal or capital gains.

The amount of the income tax deduction is found in tables

set by the U.S. Treasury. Thus, if a male donor, age sixty-five, sets up a charitable remainder annuity trust for $50,000 paying him $2,500 annually for life, he would obtain a federal income tax gift deduction of almost $30,000. The size of deduction varies with age, sex, and amount of income received.

Charitable Remainder Unitrust

This lifelong income plan differs from the annuity trust by giving the donor (and also a survivor, if wished) an annual payment determined by multiplying some agreed-upon percentage of the fair market value of the assets of the trust, revalued each year. If, for instance one chooses to receive 5 percent return on a trust fund set up with $20,000, one would receive $1,000 the first year, based on a fair market value of $20,000. If, the second year the assets are worth $25,000, one would receive $1,250. One can elect to receive a higher or lower percent of return, thereby decreasing or increasing the charitable deduction and the gift to the institution. A gift of $100,000 by a male, age sixty-five, paying 5 percent, would have a tax deduction of more than $55,000 in the year the gift was made. Other tax advantages are that the trust can be so invested that part of each payment can be taxed at lower capital gains rate.

The Pooled Income Fund

In this type of deferred gift the institution which receives the principal invests it in a pool of other similar gifts. The annual earnings of the pool are then distributed pro rata among the givers. Each one's return fluctuates year by year with the pool's earnings. U.S. Treasury tables determine the size of tax deduction in the year of the gift, varying according to age and the pool's earning experience. A two-life contract can be written.

Almost 50 percent of all of Harvard's planned gifts are in the pooled income fund. The university offers a choice of three funds: high yields paying 8 percent, balanced paying 6 percent, and growth paying 2½ percent.

Charitable Gift Annuity

In this type of gift/investment you transfer to the philanthropic organization cash or securities for which you (and survivor, if desired) are paid a fixed amount annually for life. A sizable portion of each annuity payment you receive is free of tax, which remains constant throughout life. Rates for men and women are the same. If a person age sixty-five takes an annuity, his or her annual income is 6.2 percent. There is a capital gains tax on a gift of appreciated property, though smaller than the gain if the property were sold. The gain, furthermore, is not all reportable in the year of the gift.

The Deferred Payment Gift Annuity

This type of gift is usually made before retirement, with payment of benefits to begin at retirement or later. The savings on taxes is made immediately. If the donor (man or woman) is age fifty-five, with annuity payments to begin at age sixty-five, the rate of return is 8.7 percent. This gift has the advantage of a larger charitable tax deduction when one's tax bracket is apt to be higher, along with guaranteed annual payments when one's tax bracket is apt to be lower.

Life Ownership

This gift provides for transfer of ownership of real estate to a charitable institution with lifetime use of the property. It can be a two-life contract. One receives a tax charitable deduction in the year of gift and has the same estate tax benefits as if making a bequest. Probate costs are also saved.

Charitable Lead Trust

This type of trust is quite different from the preceding trusts. The trust pays income to the charitable institution for a term of years, but at the termination the trust principal is paid over to the heirs of the donor. The charitable payout can be either a certain annual sum or a fixed percentage of the trust assets determined annually. No charitable gift deduction is allowed, but since the trust removes the assets from the donor's control, the donor pays no tax on the trust income. The trust qualifies for a 100 percent charitable income tax deduction for charitable distribution but pays taxes on any undistributed income. Should the property of the trust appreciate, the growth would benefit the heirs. The longer the term of years and the higher the rate of interest paid, the lower the value of the heirs' interest subject to tax.

Bequests

The federal government grants an estate tax charitable deduction (most states do, too). The Tax Reform Act of 1976 made many changes in estate and gift tax laws. The marital deduction was raised, and an increased exemption in the form of a credit was allowed. See your advisor for details. There remains an unlimited estate tax deduction. Estate taxes are paid, not on the gross estate, but on the taxable estate (after funeral expenses, debts, administrative expenses, and all charitable deductions). Herein lies an incentive for charitable bequests.

Bequests come to those organizations, usually, which have a program of encouraging such gifts. The program begins with a volunteer chairperson and committee, supported by a staff member. It is wise to have at least one lawyer on the committee, or a banker, or an accountant. Begin solicitation with the committee itself and then with the board of trustees. Set yourself an annual goal of bequests to be written. After committee members have made their own wills, they should begin cultivating two or three prospects personally.

Printed publicity will be essential. Perhaps a new piece should be distributed every year. It might point out the number of persons in the country who do not have wills, and the consequences thereof, including generally higher court costs and taxes. One piece could point out the goals of the committee and some projects which could be benefited. Acknowledgment of bequests made helps others to think likewise. A special packet for lawyers and trust officers to place in their files could be of eventual help.

Too often the bequest program is not implemented. This work calls for careful planning—making a prospect list, selecting a committee, preparing publicity, and agreeing on procedure.

One of the hindrances to a bequest program is the fear of lawyers or trust officers exploiting their professional relationship. It needs to be pointed out that the organization is not asking these key persons to push your work but rather to be ready to mention your cause when the client is open for suggestions. It may be that the nonprofessional becomes an even better partner in obtaining bequests, for this person can casually speak of the value of bequests in a personal way—values both to the institution and the donor. Every now and then some bizarre bequest is reported by the press. It should cause all humanitarian agencies to wonder why someone had not, at some time, dropped a gentle suggestion.

Although many persons will not speak of their wills, there may be one or two who do. Reporting of such can be helpful. Endowments are usually built of bequests. Give publicity when it happens, particularly if your group can state that it had an influence in writing the bequest.

The bequest committee should be asked to make periodic reports of progress.

There are many ways to raise funds for philanthropic causes. Most gifts are a result of research, imagination, preparation, and a willingness to ask. Some gifts come in quickly, but most (especially the larger ones) take much time. Persistence is essential.

Occasionally a munificent contribution is called a "miracle gift". But almost invariably there was some one or more persons who labored long and quietly in the background, presenting the cause and cultivating the donor-to-be.

Perhaps there is some thought—some method—some mechanic in this book that will help you in financing a commendable work. If so, the effort in bringing it to you has been worthwhile.

Bibliography

BIBLIOGRAPHIES

Foundation Center, *Bibliography of Area Foundation Directories,* (888 Seventh Avenue, New York, N.Y., 10019), 1979.

National Catholic Development Conference, *Bibliography of Fund Raising and Philanthropy,* (119 North Park Avenue, Rockville Center, N.Y., 11570), 1977, $22.50.

REFERENCE WORKS

American Association of Fund Raising Counsel, *Giving USA* (500 Fifth Avenue, New York, N.Y., 10036). Annual.

Dun and Bradstreet, *Reference Book of Corporate Managements* (New York, 1967ff.)

Martindale-Hubbell, *Law Directory.* (7 volumes, One Prospect Street, Summit, N.J., 07901).

Moody's Industrial Manual, (Moody's Investors Service, 99 Church Street, New York, N.Y., 10007), 2 volumes.

Social Registers of thirteen large cities.

Standard and Poor's *Register of Corporations, Directors, and Executives,* 3 volumes. (Annual, 25 Broadway, New York, N.Y., 10004).

Standard and Poor's *Register—Geographical Index.* (Annual, 25 Broadway, New York, N.Y. 10004).

Who's Who in America. (Chicago: Marquis Who's Who, Annual).
Who's Who in Finance and Industry. (Chicago: Marquis Who's Who, 1974–1975).

PHILOSOPHY OF FUND RAISING

Academy of Political Science, *Proceedings,* (vol. XXX, no. 1), "The Corporator and the Campus" (Columbia University, N.Y., 1970).

John H. Filer (ed.), *Commission on Private Philanthropy and Public Needs,* (Washington: The Commission, 1975). 1975.

Harvard Business Review, March/April 1971, Dan H. Fenn, Jr., "Executives As Community Volunteers."

Arnaud C. Marts, *Philanthropy's Role in Civilization,* (New York: Harper, 1953).

Harold J. Seymour, *Designs for Fund Raising,* (New York: McGraw Hill, 1966).

HISTORY OF FUND RAISING, INSTITUTIONS, AND LEADERS

E. Digby Baltzell, *Puritan Boston and Quaker Philadelphia,* (New York: Free Press, 1980).

Scott M. Cutlip, *Fund Raising in the United States: Its Role in America's Philanthropy,* (New Brunswick: Brown Book, 1965).

Foster R. Dulles, *American Red Cross, A History* (New York: Greenwood, 1950).

Raymond B. Fosdick, *The Story of the Rockefeller Foundation* (New York: Harper, 1952).

Edgar J. Goodspeed, *As I Remember,* (New York: Harper, 1953).

Thomas W. Goodspeed, *Story of the University of Chicago* (Chicago: The University of Chicago Press, 1925).

C. Howard Hopkins, *History of the YMCA in North America* (New York: Association Press, 1951).

Nathaniel R. Howard, *Trust for All Time,* a history of the Cleveland Foundation (Cleveland: Cleveland Foundation, 1963).

William Lawrence, *Memories of a Happy Life,* (Boston: Houghton Mifflin, 1926).

Samuel E. Morison, *Three Centuries of Harvard* (Cambridge: Harvard University Press, 1937).

Allan Nevins, *John D. Rockefeller* (New York: Scribner's, 1940).

Harold J. Seymour, *Design for Giving: The Story of the National War Fund* (New York: Harper, 1947).

Richard H. Shryock, *National Tuberculosis Association* (New York: Arno, 1957; also 1977).

FOUNDATIONS

American Assembly, *The Future of Foundations* (Englewood Cliffs, N.J.: Prentice-Hall, 1973).

F. Emerson Andrews, *Foundation Watcher* (Lancaster, Pa.: Franklin and Marshall Press, 1973).

F. Emerson Andrews, *Legal Instruments of Foundations* (New York: Russell Sage, 1958).

Commission of Foundations and Private Philanthropy, *Foundations: Private Giving and Public Policy* (Chicago: University of Chicago Press, 1970).

Merrimon Cuninggim, *Private Money and Public Service: The Role of Foundations in American Society* (New York: McGraw Hill, 1972).

The Foundation Center, 888 Seventh Avenue, New York, N.Y., 10019, is an independent, nonprofit organization established by foundations to provide information for the grant-seeking public. It has four national libraries: New York, Washington, Cleveland, and San Francisco. It supplies publications and resources to cooperating collections in over 80 libraries in all 50 states, Mexico, and Puerto Rico.

For the name of the library collection nearest you or for information about the center's program, call toll free (800) 424–9836. It publishes many works, of which the following are the more outstanding:

Foundation Directory, 7th Edition 1979. Describes 3,138 larger foundations. $41.50. A most essential work.

National Data Book. Descriptions of over 22,000 foundations, 2 vol. $45. Annually in November.

Foundation Grants to Individuals. Describes programs of 950 foundations which make grants to 44,000 individuals annually. 1979. $15.

Source Book Profiles. Series 1—1977/1978. Looseleaf service with in-depth analysis of 1,000 major foundations. $200. Series 2—Bimonthly 1978/1979. 500 profiles. $200. Series 3—Bimonthly 1979/1980. 500 profiles. $200.

The Foundation Grants Index. Annual listing of the grants of $5,000 or more made by 500 major foundations. Subject index to over 12,000 grants per year. Annually in April. $27.

Foundation Fundamentals: A Guide for Grantseekers, Carol M. Kurzig, 1980.

COMSEARCH Printouts. Computer printouts listing grants in 59 subject areas by more than 300 foundations. $11 per subject ($3 per microfiche). Annually in April.

International Philanthropy. Index to more than 900 international grants of major foundations. $35.

About Foundations: How to Find the Facts You Need to Get a Grant, Judith B. Margolin, $5.

Foundation Annual Reports: What They Are and How to Use Them, Henry G. Russell. A listing of about 400 foundations which publish reports. $3.

Philanthropy in the United States: History and Structure, F. Emerson Andrews. $1.50.

The Foundation Center provides several brief pamphlets free of charge, up to five copies.

The Associates Program provides special services to fund raisers with a continuing need for information on foundations. Annual fee of $200 entitles associates to toll free telephone reference service, access to computerized data bases, duplicating service, and library research service.

Marion R. Fremont-Smith, *Foundations and Government: State and Federal Law and Supervision* (New York: Russell Sage Foundation, 1965).

Joseph C. Goulden, *The Money Givers* (New York: Random House, 1971). A criticism of foundations.

George G. Kirstein, *Better Giving: The New Needs of American Philanthropy* (Boston: Houghton Mifflin, 1975). An appraisal and criticism of causes and methods.

Waldemar A. Nielsen, *The Big Foundations.* A Twentieth Century study. Critical examination of the 33 largest foundations. (New York: Columbia University Press, 1972).

John M. Russell, *Giving and Taking; Across the Foundation Desk* (New York: Teachers College, 1977).

Russell Sage Foundation, *Foundations—20 Viewpoints* (New York: Russell Sage Foundation, 1965).

Warren Weaver, *U.S. Philanthropic Foundations: Their History, Structure, Management, and Record* (New York: Harper & Row, 1967).

Ben Whitaker, *The Philanthropoids: Foundations and Society* (New York: Morrow, 1974).

Arnold J. Zurcher, *Management of America's Foundations: Adminis-*

tration, Policies, and Social Role (New York: New York University Press, 1972).

FUND RAISING
MANUALS AND AIDS

Karen Abarbanel and Howard Hillman, *The Art of Winning Foundation Grants* (New York: Vanguard Press, 1975). $6.95.

Annual Register of Grant Support, Marquis Academic Media (200 E. Ohio Street, Chicago, Il., 60611). $55.

A Guide to Federal Funding in the Arts and Humanities, Federal Resources Advisory Service of the Association of American Colleges, 1818 R Street, N.W., Washington, D.C., 20009. $7.50.

The Fund Raising Institute, Box 122, Plymouth Meeting, Pa., 19462
Fund Raising Letter Collection $25.
Complete Handbook for Fund Raisers $12.50
Bequest Program Handbook $10.
Foundations Portfolio $7.50.
Publicity Portfolio $5.

The Bread Game, Glide Publications, 330 Ellis Street, San Francisco, Calif., 94102, 1973. $2.95.

Mary Hall, *Developing Skills in Proposal Writing,* Continuing Education Publications, Waldo Hall 100, Corvallis, Ore., 97331. 1972. $10.

Howard Hillman, *The Art of Winning Government Grants,* (New York: Vanguard Press, 1977).

Howard Hillman, *Art of Winning Corporate Grants* (New York: Vanguard Press, 1979).

Robert Lefferts, *Getting a Grant: How to Write Successful Grant Proposals,* (Englewood Cliffs, N.J.: Prentice-Hall, 1978).

Manual of Practical Fund Raising, Massachusetts VITA, 294 Washington Street, Boston, Mass., 02108. 1975. $2.50.

Public Service Materials Center, 355 Lexington Avenue, New York, N.Y., 10017.
Joseph Dermer, *Where America's Large Foundations Make Their Grants,* 1977, $24.
Joseph Dermer, *The New How to Raise Funds from Foundations,* 1975. $8.95.
Joseph Dermer, *How to Write Successful Foundation Presentations,* 1975. $8.95.
Philip Des Marais, *How to Get Government Grants,* $13.50.
How to Get Your Fair Share of Foundation Grants, 1973. $12.

199

The 1976–1977 Survey of Grant-Making Foundations. $8.50.

Howard R. Mirkin, *The Complete Fund Raising Guide,* 1972.

Paul H. Schneiter, *The Art of Asking* (New York: Walker and Co., 1978).

Taft Products, Inc., 1000 Vermont Avenue, N.W., Washington, D.C., 20005:

> Jean Brodsky, *The Proposal Writer's Swipe File,* $5.50.
>
> Jean Brodsky, *Foundation Reporter.*
>
> Jean Brodsky, *Trustees of Wealth.*
>
> *Corporate Foundation Directory,* Reports on more than 300 corporate foundations. $90.75.
>
> *Prospecting: Searching Out the Philanthropic Dollar,* 1978.

Gerald S. Soroker, *Fund Raising for Philanthropy.* $9.95.

Bernard P. Taylor, *Guide to Successful Fund Raising.* Groups Work Today, 1976.

Lois A. Urgo, *Models for Money: Obtaining Government and Foundation Grants and Assistance,* Suffolk University, Boston, Mass., 1978.

Irving R. Warner, *The Art of Fund Raising* (New York: Harper & Row, 1975).

Virginia White, *Grants: How to Find Out About Them,* (New York: Plenum Pub., 1975). $19.50.

CORPORATION GIVING

The Council on Financial Aid to Education, 680 Fifth Avenue, New York, N.Y., 10019, encourages and supplies guidelines for corporate support of higher education. Sample titles available include:

> *The CFAE Casebook,* 1974. $9.
>
> *Guidelines for Corporate Support of Higher Education,* 1975. $2.
>
> *How Corporations Can Aid Colleges and Universities,* 1974. $2.
>
> *How to Develop and Administer a Corporate Gift-Matching Program,* 1977. $2.
>
> *How to Develop and Administer a Corporate Scholarship Program,* 1975. $2.

Richard Eells, *The Corporation and the Arts* (New York: Interbook Inc., 1967).

Marion R. Fremont-Smith, *Philanthropy and the Business Corporation* (New York: Russell Sage Foundation, 1972).

HIGHER EDUCATION AND RELIGION

Council for Advancement and Support of Education (CASE), One Dupont Circle, Suite 530–600, Washington, D.C., 20036. CASE provides many publications and other resources for educational institutions. Sample titles include:
Deferred Giving Programs: Administration and Promotion, 1972. $2.50.
Motivations for Charitable Giving: A Reference Guide. With bibliography. 1973. $5.
Involving Alumni and Parents in Fund Raising, 1975. $2.
Council on Financial Aid to Education. See section on CORPORATION GIVING.
Merle Curti and Roderick Nash, *Philanthropy in the Shaping of American Higher Education* (New Brunswick, N.J.: Rutgers University Press, 1965).
Directory of the Major Foundations Supporting Education, J. F. Gray Company, Westwood, Mass., 1975.
David R. Holt, II, *Handbook of Church Finance* (New York: Macmillan, 1960).
Othniel A. Pendleton, *New Techniques for Church Fund Raising* (New York: McGraw Hill, 1955).
J. A. Pollard, *Fund Raising for Higher Education* (New York: Harper, 1958).

DEFERRED GIVING AND TAXES

Conrad Teitel, *Deferred Giving—Explanation, Specimen Agreements, Reporting Forms,* Taxwise Giving, 13 Arcadia Road, Old Greenwich, Conn., 06870. 2 vol., 1980. $185.

GOVERNMENT PUBLICATIONS—See also PERIODICALS

Catalog of Federal Domestic Assistance, U.S. Office of Management and Budget. Government Printing Office (Washington, D.C., 20402), $20 a year. Official compendium of federal programs, projects, services, and activities providing benefits to American institutions and individuals.

Federal Assistance Programs Retrieval System, (Enhanced Version). The FAPRS is a computerized question and answer system giving rapid access to information in the Catalog. It relates 20 categories and 176 subcategories to specific areas of interest and sets forth 16 types of assistance provided by Federal programs. For location of nearest access point in your state, write to:

> Office of Management and Budget
> Budget Review Division
> Federal Program Information Branch
> Washington, D.C. 20503

Catalog of Federal Education Assistance Programs. Government Printing Office. (Washington, D.C., 20402).

Profile of Grant Programs: Public Health Service, Department of Health, Education, and Welfare, Government Printing Office (Washington D.C., 20402).

Internal Revenue Service Returns. Private foundations are required each year to file information returns with IRS—Forms 990 and 990AR. These are available for inspection at Foundation Center libraries or can be purchased from:

> Internal Revenue Service Center
> Box 187
> Cornwell Heights, Pa., 19020

PERIODICALS AND NEWSLETTERS. See also: GOVERNMENT PUBLICATIONS

CSA Upward, Community Services Administration, Office of Public Affairs (Washington, D.C., 20506).

Foundation News, Council on Foundations, 1828 L Street, N.W., Washington, D.C., 20036. Provides bimonthly update to Foundation Grants Index—Annual.

Cultural Post, National Endowment for the Arts, Washington, D.C., 20506.

Federal Grants Reporter, 2120 L Street, N.W., Washington, D.C., 20037. $85 a year.

FRI Newsletter, The Fund Raising Institute, Box 365, Ambler, Pa., 19002.

Fund Raising Management, Hoke Communications, Inc., 224 Seventh Street, Garden City, N.Y., 11530. Bimonthly, $20 a year.

Grantsmanship Center News, Grantsmanship Center, 1031 South Grand Avenue, Los Angeles, Calif., 90015. Bimonthly. $15 a year. The center is a nonprofit, tax exempt, educational institution. It supplies information on both governmental and foundation funding sources and conducts one week training programs in many cities.

HR News, Health Resources Administration, Office of Public Affairs, Hyattsville, Md., 20872.

Humanities, National Endowment for the Humanities, Washington, D.C., 20506.

LRC-W Newsbriefs, Lutheran Resources Commission, Suite 823, 1346 Connecticut Avenue, Washington, D.C., 20036.

Non-Profit Report: The Philanthropy Monthly, Non-Profit Report, 205 Main Street, Danbury, Cn., 06810. $72 a year.

The Philanthropy Monthly, Box 989, New Milford, Cn., 06776.

News Monitor of Philanthropy, Taft Products, Inc., 1000 Vermont Avenue, Washington, D.C., 20005.

Women and Foundations/Corporate Philanthropy, 866 U.N. Plaza, New York, N.Y., 10017.

Index